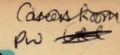
HAVING IT ALL

Make Your Life What **You**
Want It To Be

LINDA B. STOKER

B L O O M S B U R Y

Never Give Up on a Dream

If there's doubt and you're cold
Don't you worry what the future holds
We got to have heroes to teach us all
To never give up on a dream.

Written By Rod Stewart, Jim Cregan, Bernie Taupin 1981

Dedicated to: Terry Fox, Canadian Cancer Society

First published 1991 by Bloomsbury Publishing Limited, 2 Soho Square, London W1V 5DE

Copyright © 1991 by Linda B. Stoker

The moral right of the author has been asserted

British Library Cataloguing in Publication Data

A CIP record for this book is available from the British Library

ISBN 0 7475 0881 X

Designed by Geoff Green
Typeset by Rowland Phototypesetting Limited, Bury St Edmunds, Suffolk
Printed by Clays Limited, St Ives plc

Contents

To my children, Emma and Kimberley, who have played a major part in my achieving my personal goals, and who question and argue about most things — so I can never be too complacent.

To Helen, who has loved and supported me and my children since they were born.

To Sally, who perseveres with me at work and who has typed and contributed to this book.

To everyone who works for Dow-Stoker, for their hard work, love and support, and to Alan who helped when I was stuck for words.

Introduction

The title of this book states clearly that it's for women thinking about returning to work. But it's really wider-ranging than that – there's something here for everyone (and not necessarily just women) who wants to make some positive change in their lives. What you will be reading is a guide to helping you become more confident and better able to choose your direction in life.

My own life has been a series of beginnings and ends. The fact that you have bought this book is a beginning. You've decided that you haven't got everything you need in your life; perhaps you haven't even begun to think about how you could change things. If you want to make some changes, you need to be prepared to understand that most of the changes you make are going to be within yourself.

I firmly believe that most human beings are capable of most things, and that includes you. Most of the things we don't achieve are because of the limits that we set for ourselves or the limits someone else has set for us and we have accepted. As Richard Bach, author of *Jonathan Livingstone Seagull*, said, 'Argue for your limitations and sure enough they are yours!' It took me until the age of thirty to realize that I could achieve at least some of my dreams. For some people it takes a lot longer; and yet others spend their whole lives never realizing that they were actually in control and were not totally powerless.

Once that realization has taken place, you need to work out an action plan of how you are going to move ahead. I am still learning, developing within my own action plan – some days flat on my face in the mud and others picking myself back up again. I understand that I am not perfect, but I am striving to be a good example to my family, to

1

my peers, to my clients and most of all to me. Life may never be absolutely ideal, but I do know that I am heading in the right direction. I am realistic enough to know that I'll never completely get there but will have a lot of joy on the way.

At the time of writing, my company, Dow-Stoker, is a business providing training services to companies and individuals; and it will be a lot bigger in the future. Many people have asked me how I built this business. One of the keys is the techniques applied in this book. Like everyone else I have read books about charismatic, successful people such as Anita Roddick and Richard Branson, but you never really get the answers about how it's done. This book is designed to be honest, to be a true guide into how you too can 'have it all', whatever your 'all' may be.

Linda Stoker

How do you feel today?

Put a circle round the faces that best describe you at this moment.

HOW DO YOU FEEL TODAY?

Aggressive	Agonized	Anxious	Apologetic	Arrogant	Bashful	Blissful
Bored	Cautious	Cold	Concentrating	Confident	Curious	Demure
Determined	Disappointed	Disapproving	Disbelieving	Disgusted	Distasteful	Eavesdropping
Ecstatic	Enraged	Envious	Exasperated	Exhausted	Frightened	Frustrated
Grieving	Guilty	Happy	Horrified	Hot	Hungover	Helpless
Hysterical	Indifferent	Idiotic	Innocent	Interested	Jealous	Joyful
Loaded	Lonely	Lovestruck	Meditative	Mischievous	Miserable	Negative
Obstinate	Optimistic	Pained	Paranoid	Perplexed	Prudish	Regretful
Relieved	Sad	Satisfied	Shocked	Sheepish	Smug	Surly
Surprised	Suspicious	Sympathetic	Thoughtful	Undecided	Withdrawn	Other

Notes

1   **The Balancing Act**

One of the first questions that any woman returner asks herself is this: Will I be able to balance the demands of my job with my responsibilities at home?

If you have spent some years at home bringing up children, you've had to get things well organized. However, much of that organization usually means that you do it yourself. If you now go back to work there are going to be fewer hours in the day to get things done.

What could other people do for you? Make a list here:

-
-
-
-
-
-
-

Who else would do it if you weren't around? Write their names here:

-
-
-

What training would they need to do it to *your* standards? The simplest formula for training is:

- I do it (demonstrate)
- You do it with me (I coach you)
- You do it alone (you tell me how you did – we fine-tune mistakes)

Childcare

There are many solutions to managing childcare. Playgroups usually only cater for children doing either a morning or afternoon session and do like you to be on hand and join in if necessary. There are only thirty thousand nursery places available for children in Britain, so if you have a young baby and are thinking of going back to work later on, it's best to put your name down now!

Childminders can be one of the better solutions if they are close by and can become a friend of the family. However, you need to take into consideration that childminders are not trained and do not have any actual qualifications for looking after your child. On the other hand they may be mature and experienced people.

More companies are considering the provision of workplace nurseries for their staff. However, very few have actually yet put this idea into practice.

Some other suggestions are:

- Local council provision – many towns do try to provide some sort of nursery provision, and may also be able to offer holiday play schemes or holiday play centres.
- Au pairs – if you have a spare bedroom in your house an au pair may be a good idea. Au pairs can work in Britain if they are from any EC country or from a non-EC country if they plan to learn English combined with looking after your children. However, au pairs can be very young and inexperienced at looking after children.
- Nannies – they often command high salaries but will be trained and have college qualifications. (The qualifications obtained by nannies may be from the NNEB or City and Guilds. Check the meaning of any qualifications with the library or local college. Don't forget to ask what the person covered during the course.) They too may be rather young and not have the length of experience that you would prefer. Why not ask at the local technical college if they have a training programme for nannies, and invite

some of them to come and gain work experience with you and your child? You may just find the sort of person you are looking for.

- Sharing a nanny – because of the high cost of a nanny it's sometimes easier to share one with a friend who also wants to go back to work.

Being let down on childcare

A recent study showed that 50 per cent of Britain's children are looked after by fathers or grandparents. Many women are able to timetable their working day in conjunction with their partner, in order to organize childcare arrangements between them amicably. However, you do need to decide what time you will allow yourself back at work. Will this be part-time? Will you need to work flexi-time? Can you find a company who can offer you school hours, term-time working or even home working?

What happens in a crisis?

If you can negotiate assertively with your family (for help on this, see Chapter 5), you may be able to reorganize the daily routine so others take a share. However, just when you think things are going well, normally there is a disaster! The children are sick, the cooker explodes in the kitchen, the car breaks down in the middle of nowhere. What happens then?

The best way to deal with this is to think of all the worst things that could go wrong and plan what you would do in a crisis, how you could share responsibility and make sure that people can be easily reached. As a mum you should not be the only person who has the telephone number of the school, the doctor, etc. and that your partner is not the only person who knows how to reach a plumber or his parents.

Back-to-work crisis checklist

	Name	Telephone
People to look after children at short notice:		
Doctor:		
Dentist:		
School:		
Playschool/nursery:		
Parents – mine:		
Parents – my partner's:		
Employer – mine:		
Employer – my partner's:		
Plumber:		
Electrician:		
Gas:		
Water:		
Insurance companies:		
Garage:		
Others in case of emergency for me or a childminder:		

-
-
-

Travelling time

Most women working in a non-professional or non-managerial post will be willing to travel up to half an hour from door to door, home to work. If taking a more senior position most women will give up as much as an hour a day to travel each way. This needs to be well timetabled so as to dovetail with whatever new domestic arrangements you are setting up.

Running the home in a different way

Bearing all these points in mind, here are two questionnaires to set you off in the right direction and help you to balance the demands of work, home and family.

How much you get out of this book depends on how much you put in. The more effort you put into working through the questions as they apply to you, the more insights you will get. If you can, try to discuss your answers with someone else after you have completed each part.

Whatever you did or didn't do in a job, and however long ago it was, you will in the meantime have gained experience in many areas that can later apply to work. We'll look more closely at these 'transferable skills' in Chapter 2, but first let's look at what you do in your day and how you might be able to reorganize it to give you time to go back to work.

Do you do any of these?	How will these be organized in the future?
Domestic chores: cleaning; cooking; washing, etc.	
Care of children and/or dependent relatives	
Shopping	
Preparing/cooking meals	
Washing/ironing/mending	
Household decorations and repairs	
Gardening	
Driving	
Negotiating with: your children's school(s); other public bodies	
Organizing special occasions: parties; fetes etc.	
Voluntary work (please list)	

Now look back at your answers. Are you happy with them? If not, what needs to change? If you are stuck on how to change things, turn to the section on assertiveness (p. 80).

Combining family and work

Think about your commitments at home. Do they have any effect on the hours you can work and the distance you can travel?

Hours of work

Let's have a look at how your present situation affects your ability to go back to work. Have a go at the next set of questions. These questions will almost certainly be asked by a prospective employer, so you need to think out your answers in advance in order to make a good impression.

	Now	If you could arrange care of children or dependants
What would be the earliest starting time for work?		
What would be the lastest starting time for work?		
What would be the maximum length of your working day?		
How much time would you need for lunch?		
Could you work irregular hours if necessary?		
How many days a week could you work?		
Could you work Saturdays if necessary? How about Sunday?		
How many weeks' holiday a year would you need?		
Do you have to take holiday during school holidays?		
Which areas could you travel to?		

Managing yourself

Managing home and work also means managing yourself. And that means:

1. Taking regular exercise – have you thought about going to the local gym? The instructors there will be sympathetic and helpful even if you are well out of condition, and if you don't want anyone to see what shape you are, wear a large baggy T-shirt!
2. Make sure that you get enough sleep and rest. Some people find that, although they feel tired, they cannot sleep. Establishing a regular bedtime will help. Go to bed when you feel tired, even if it is earlier than normal.
3. Eating well. There is a saying that if we eat junk food on the run we may well look like junk ourselves and certainly won't be able to run! Be sure that you get a balanced diet which includes:
   - Protein – meat, fish, cheese, pulses or eggs
   - Carbohydrate – bread, rice, potatoes, pasta
   - Vitamins and minerals in the form of fresh vegetables and fresh fruit
   - Fats, especially oily fish – herring, tuna, etc.

There are many opinions on what you should and should not eat. The best advice is to try to eat as much fresh food as possible and don't overindulge on anything. Have a little of everything. Check your weight for your height with your doctor, and if necessary cut down a little until you reach the right weight.

However, dieting is not enough on its own to keep you in good shape – you also need to exercise. Half an hour a day is enough – so long as it is the right type of exercise. Try swimming, walking or cycling to begin with.

The other things you need to manage yourself well will also be discussed later in this book. They include having some private time, managing stress and building relationships, as well as developing a positive attitude. All these will be important in helping you balance your work and your home life.

Notes on Chapter 1

2 Taking Stock

What do you want out of life?

Your wants in life need to be your own. When we are children everyone has expectations of us. What, for example, did your parents want you to do when you grew up? And for that matter, how about your grandparents, brothers and sisters, teachers and friends?

I remember my mother wanting me to be a personal assistant to a managing director. This was what *she* had achieved, and indeed in the 1950s when she was at work it was an enviable position for a woman. She never dreamed that I would become a managing director!

My first job was as a shorthand typist – I was fired after three days, mainly for poor spelling. My main sin was mis-spelling 'Majorca'. It was not in the dictionary, and at that time not many people had actually visited the island. My second sin was being too wrapped up in my boyfriend, who was definitely a moody character.

My second job was as a secretary. After about four weeks my boss said, 'Well, I'm either going to have to fire you or promote you.'

My reply was, 'Oh, please promote me – I was fired *last* time!'

He did – promote me, that is.

At that stage in my life, I had had no real careers guidance and had very little idea of what I wanted to do or what I was capable of. This guide is designed to help you make some of those fundamental decisions about your life.

If you are just starting out again on a career or even just looking for a 'job', the next exercise is to help you. You may be unhappy with the work you are doing now. About 30 per cent of the women I've met through our training courses are certainly in this position. You might

13

also be looking to improve relationships with someone or even your present situation. Common examples are people who have said to me:

- 'I just want to feel better about my self-image – maybe lose some weight.'
- 'I'd really like to take control of my life – give up smoking.'

Now here is your opportunity to make some new plans. Let's have a look at how you manage your time at the moment and how you'd like to reorganize it for the future.

How do you spend your time?

Time is one of our most valuable commodities. We have only a very limited amount of it on this planet, and to get the most from your life you need to fill it fruitfully. If we had five hundred years on earth we could say, 'OK, I'll spend the first hundred years doing nothing in particular, the next hundred learning about life, the next hundred building a relationship, the next hundred working and my last hundred in leisure.' We don't have that amount of time, yet very few people feel the urgency to get it right. Here's an exercise to help you identify how you're spending your time now.

If the average life expectancy is about seventy years, how many years have you got left now and how are you going to get the most from them?

STEP 1   List in column 1 everything you've done in the last three days. Add other things that you should have done or wanted to do.

STEP 2   Now try to decide how you feel about each task. Is it:
- A = urgent and important
- B = important and non-urgent
- C = urgent and unimportant
- D = non-urgent and unimportant

STEP 3   From your time sheet covering three typical days add up the amount of time you've spent on all these activities/jobs.

STEP 4   How much time should have been allocated to that job/ activity? Did you spend:
- Too little time
- Too long
- Should someone else have done it?

Timesheet

Activities (job or home)	Grade A–D	Actual time it took	Time it should have taken	Difference	How I want to change things
1.					
2.					
3.					
4.					
5.					
6.					
7.					
8.					
9.					
10.					
11.					
12.					

(Use another sheet if necessary)

Changes I now need to make

If you've taken the last exercise seriously, you'll be able to list some changes you'd like to make:

```



```

Go on – have a go! Don't leave a blank space here – no one's life is perfect.

Now let's take a look at talents and abilities you already possess and which can be adapted to new uses in whatever new direction you want your life to take.

Skills you never knew you had

The average time away from work for a woman who leaves to raise a family is eight years, and 30 per cent of women attending the Dow-Stoker Returners courses have been away from the workplace for over fifteen years. It is hardly surprising, therefore, that many women returners are confused about what kind of job to look for.

In this situation, it is often useful to look back at the good things you have achieved and the good times you've enjoyed in the past. Identifying these will often give you some ideas about the path you would most like to take in the future.

Also, by looking at the activities you are good at and enjoy you may well discover talents and abilities which you have not considered before as being useful in a job. For instance, you may think that running a household and looking after your children is all in a day's work; however, the planning skills needed to do this could be a very useful quality to have in some jobs.

So in this chapter you will find some pointers for looking at what you might think are everyday activities. These will enable you to assess for yourself what your strengths and weaknesses are, as well as the areas in which you might like to consider working in the future.

First thoughts

Write here your first thoughts about returning to work. Here are a few words to start you off: underline the ones that apply to you:

EASY   DIFFICULT   STIMULATING   BORING

AFRAID   HOPEFUL   HOPELESS   LITTLE TO OFFER

LOOKING FORWARD   LOTS TO OFFER

Your words here:

What am I good at?

Listed below are eight types of skill. Have a look to see whether these things apply to you – it is not a test. Just try to decide what things you consider yourself to be good at. After this section you will have a summary table to fill in so you can see your answers at a glance.

	This sounds like me	This is not me
I Verbal and written skills		
1. I am able to explain things well so that others understand		
2. I have a wide vocabulary, which I am continually expanding, so I often look up the meaning of words to use		
3. I am able to summarize something that someone has written or said.		
4. I am rarely lost for words to say what I mean		
5. I like to write poetry, stories or letters		
6. I like doing puzzles that involve words		
7. I use the library, or regularly buy books or magazines		
II Numerical ability		
8. I'm good at number puzzles		
9. I can work out the family budget easily		
10. I can work out how much I have in my bank account		
11. I find it quite easy to understand information using numbers, such as tables, accounts, technical data, graphs or statistics		
12. I always know if I've been given the wrong change		
13. I'm good at maths, technical and practical subjects		

	This sounds like me	This is not me
14. I enjoy working things out with numbers, e.g. how much wallpaper or carpet I need to buy		

III Spatial ability

15. I like to navigate using a map when going somewhere new in a car		
16. I can make a pattern for a dress or for cake decoration		
17. I like to draw a diagram or chart rather than write or talk about something		
18. I can plan out how furniture will fit into a room		
19. I am often congratulated when I draw a map for someone of how to reach somewhere		
20. I can plan a new kitchen easily, i.e. where all the cupboards and appliances would fit		
21. If I decorate I always buy the right amount of paint		

IV Memory

22. I can remember faces		
23. I can remember names		
24. I can remember telephone numbers		
25. I can recall events		
26. I can remember conversations		
27. I can remember what I did on the first day of my holiday last year		
28. I can remember my last schoolteacher's name		

V Observation

29. I can pick out a face in a crowd or a name on a list		
30. I can do difficult jigsaws		
31. I notice things which other people often miss		

	This sounds like me	This is not me
32. From a general mass of information I can usually pick out the precise thing I'm looking for		
33. I can find things quickly at the library		
34. I can spot errors in the newspaper		
35. I can remember details about people – what they were wearing, hairstyle, etc.		

VI Reason

36. I know when what I have said is not logical		
37. I'm good at logic puzzles, like those where you have to find a code from jumbled letters		
38. I can tell if someone contradicts themselves		
39. I am good at TV 'whodunnits'		
40. I am good at quizzes that involve logic		
41. People say I am logical		
42. My family bring me problems to solve because I can see both sides of the argument		

VII Innovation and ideas

43. I am usually able to come up with an idea		
44. I am innovative and can think of new ways of using old materials, such as making toys from everyday household items		
45. I don't imitate what other people have done		
46. If I have a problem I can often think of more than one way to deal with it		
47. I often come up with an idea and keep it for later		

	This sounds like me	This is not me
48. I could think of a way to feed a family of four on 50 pence each or less		
49. People often bring me their problems to solve		

VIII Practical abilities

50. I like to do practical jobs around the house		
51. Making and fitting curtains is something that I am good at		
52. I find it easy to do electrical repairs, e.g. mending fuses/fitting plugs		
53. I can make children's clothes		
54. I knit very well, and do not make mistakes		
55. I can hang wallpaper and make a success of it		
56. I like to paint the house		

Summary

Here's a summary, which shows you how each of these strengths can be made use of in the workplace. The questionnaire contained seven questions in each section; look at those where you scored highest. It's only a rough guide, so, after reading the definition of each category, look also at those abilities which you feel are strongest in you. Rank your best area (1) and the others in order of importance up to (8).

Abilities

	Definition	Rank 1–8
Verbal and written skills	To understand both the spoken and written communication and to say what you mean accurately	
Numerical ability	To understand and use numbers at work	
Spatial ability	Distances, spaces and shapes	
Memory	Good recent and long-term memory	
Observation	To understand events around you	
Reason	To understand logic at work	
Innovation and ideas	To be able to be creative and innovative and use ideas	
Practical abilities	To make or work things with your hands	

Adapting your skills to the job market

You may now be thinking about what sorts of jobs you could do if you score high in any of the areas that we've mentioned.

Verbal and written skills

You may feel that you were good at English or school or have a flair for the English language. There are a number of careers in which written English is central to the job, for example:

- Advertising copywriter
- Editor
- Journalist
- Speech therapist

Jane was thirty-three and had two children, one of whom had a slight speech defect which made Jane very interested in speech therapy. She also had a great interest in the English language and a strong desire to work with people. She found out about the work and discovered that it needed understanding and patience and was very demanding; speech therapists have to be effective communicators, with clear and accurate speech, a sensitive ear and a good command of written English.

There were lots of different people to deal with and the ability to gain the confidence of patients was essential. She also found that her driving licence would be handy and she sometimes needed to visit patients at home. Jane had English and biology A-levels, but she found that anyone could enrol as a mature student for training in speech therapy; however, entry to courses is becoming increasingly competitive.

Jane went back to college and took a degree course. After this she managed to get a job in the National Health Service, where the majority of speech therapists are employed.

For people who score highly in this area there are also many other careers in which English has a strong bearing. These range from archivist to VDU (visual display unit, or computer screen) operator. Here are a few more:

- Administrative assistant in the Civil Service
- Barrister's clerk
- Broadcasting floor manager
- Building surveyor
- Court reporter
- Employment agency interviewer
- Health Service manager
- Interpreter
- Librarian
- Market research executive
- Personnel officer
- Psychologist
- Receptionist
- Retail manager
- Trading standards officer
- Travel agent

Numerical ability

There are very few careers in which you can use solely numerical ability, unless of course you become a statistician or schoolteacher.

However, this subject is most important to us at school because there are so many jobs on which it has a bearing, ranging from accountant to town planner.

Mary was forty-six and had left school without any educational qualifications. However, on a Dow-Stoker Returners programme she discovered that she had quite a strong numerical ability, and decided that she would like to work in an accounts department. She found that accounts and finance clerks deal with tasks such as:

- Costing – calculating the overall cost of an item or service by working out the costs of labour, materials and overheads
- Invoicing – making out and checking invoices and keeping accurate records
- Ledger work – writing out the transactions carried out by a company in a day book, book-keeping and sometimes calculating the staff wages

Mary was a stickler for accuracy, which is really needed in this job; you also need a lot of patience to tackle it effectively. She joined an insurance company, which trained her as an accounts clerk. When they introduced computers they also taught her typing and keyboard skills.

Nearly every organization requires accounts or finance clerks, so if mathematics is your strong point it is something to think about. If Mary wishes to she can go on and train to be an accountant; the qualifying body for this is the Chartered Association of Certified Accounts (CACA). Candidates over twenty-five may be allowed to enrol if they have obtained a position of responsibility in a non-accounting career – that means that you won't necessarily need A-levels to do the course. Courses can be part-time or full-time.

Further information can be gained from the Chartered Institute for Certified Accountants, 29 Lincoln's Inn Fields, London WC2A 3EE.

Spatial ability

There are a number of careers in which looking at distance, shape and space and the way they interact is important. One of these jobs is as a draughtsperson. These people prepare diagrams, drawings and plans of a technical nature and are employed at two levels, design and detail.

In the former you examine design specifications from which are produced a drawing, diagram or plan to scale, looking at the most economic and effective way of manufacturing the article. This does require advanced technical skills.

Detail is a lower-level job, involving the preparation of detailed drawings for use by craftsmen or women. It can involve redrawing the work to show a different scale of projection, or breaking it down into a general drawing or a series of drawings.

Computers are now being brought into this profession to perform repetitive tasks. Mathematical skills will also be important here, although artistic skills are not particularly necessary.

You can join at three levels. Adults can apply for BTEC (Business and Technology Education Council) or SCOTBEC (Scottish Business Education Council) courses, and there are some government-sponsored training schemes, mainly for craft level. Craft-level courses are equivalent to what would have been apprenticeship level. Some of the courses require O-levels, but mature students are often accepted without any qualifications.

Memory

A good memory is necessary in so many different jobs. Sally found that she had good abilities in this area. She had been away from work for eight years and her second child was starting school when she saw an advertisement for a part-time market research executive. The job asked for someone to collect information about consumer needs, carry out surveys using questionnaires and interviews, and organize and present the data for analysis. Someone else would then interpret the data and write reports.

Sally had previously worked in the sales department of a large food manufacturing company. She found that her experience in advertising and selling was an advantage. Because the job is only part-time Sally can do it whilst the children are at school. She is thinking of taking a course run by the Market Research Society so that she can expand her career.

If you are interested in working in this area, the society's address is 15 Belgrave Square, London SW1X 8PS.

Observation

This is another skill which is used in a variety of jobs and careers, ranging from broadcasting production research assistant to quantity surveyor.

Wendy had worked at a local hospital as a clerk in medical records before giving up work to look after her children. With those children now at secondary school she wanted to restart her career and decided that she would like to become a dental hygienist. However, she found that there was too much competition for the small number of places available on training courses.

Dental hygienists work independently in a dental surgery, giving treatment such as scaling and polishing teeth; they also try to educate people to try to take better care of their teeth. Wendy managed to get a job as a receptionist in a dental surgery to begin with and will keep applying for one of the hygienist training courses.

More information is available from the British Hygienist Association, 64 Wimpole Street, London W1M 8AL.

Reason

If you were ever interested in sociology, psychology or community studies, there are many jobs in which you could use your reasoning abilities. Some examples are:

- Dietician
- Journalist
- Local government clerk
- Prison officer
- Nurse

Val had four children aged between seventeen and six, and had been working as a childminder at home to supplement the family income. However, once the youngest had started school she found she wanted to do much more. The local hospital was offering nursing training courses; however, the first year these were available Val applied too late, so she became a nursing auxiliary instead. This meant she had to help patients with personal hygiene, dressing and undressing them, and assisting in feeding them; she also got involved in weighing patients, taking samples and temperatures, and helping prepare patients for operations as well as making snacks and beds. No formal or academic qualifications were required for this, and she did get some training.

The next year she applied for the nursing course. Val was thirty-eight, and was glad that there was no age limit on the entry for the course. During the first year she didn't have to work nights. Now she is in her second year and is expected to become a Registered General Nurse (RGN).

Val enjoys her work; her husband, who is a milkman, is able to tie in his shifts with hers at the hospital so that there is always someone to look after the children.

Innovation and ideas

Any job that doesn't need your ideas is probably not worth having. However there are some that definitely require you to think of new ways to do things. Designer and architect are probably the most demanding of these skills, although it could be argued that artists and writers, beauty consultants, hairdressers and photographers also need them.

Christine had trained as a hairdresser before stopping work to have her two children. She now works for herself part-time as a mobile hairdresser, undertaking work at home or in her clients' own homes. Hairdressers have generally undertaken an apprenticeship; however, some colleges have places for mature students and there is nothing to stop you working from home. Christine certainly needs a lot of physical stamina as she is on her feet all day long.

Hairdressers can get advice from the Hairdressing Training Board, Silver House, 17 Silver Street, Doncaster, South Yorkshire.

Practical

If you are a practical type of person, there are many careers you could follow. These range from architectural technician and aerial rigger to window-dresser or wood machinist. Let's have a look at just some of these.

- Aircraft engineer – the main employers include civilian airlines. You will need to take a craft or technician apprenticeship.
- Ceramics glazer or painter/decorator – this work involves glazing and decorating pottery. You will need to be able to work for long periods with a high degree of accuracy, and have really good eyesight. Training is usually on the job and the main employers are the large commercial potteries concentrated in the North Stafford-shire area, although there is nothing to stop you working for yourself at home.
- Computer service engineer – installing and maintaining computer systems and carrying out repairs when breakdowns occur. Full-time courses are available, including electronic computer technology and telecommunications. There are some government-sponsored training schemes available. For more in-

formation contact the Engineering Careers Information Service, PO Box 176, 54 Clarendon Road, Watford, Herts WD1 1LD. You could also contact the Society of Electronic and Radio Technicians, 57–61 Newington Causeway, London SE1 6BL, tel. (071) 403 2351.

- Florist – if you are gifted in this area you may not need training. However, most adult education classes will include something on flower arranging and many colleges provide courses on floristry. There is a florist's shop in nearly every town; nowadays large stores too are selling more plants and may look for your services in the retail sector.

- Plumber – more women are taking on what used to be traditionally male jobs, mainly because they are better paid. Plumbing is one area where women can be successful. Adults can be eligible for apprenticeships in this area and information can be obtained from the Construction Industry Training Board (CITB), Careers Advisory Service, Bircham Newton, Kings Lynn, Norfolk, TE31 6RH.

Applying for training or retraining

Here are some examples of how to apply for courses: these are all letters received by Dow-Stoker. Be as clear and concise as you can, not concealing your shortcomings (age, time spent away from the workplace, and so on) but equally making the most of your qualifications, experience and other assets. See p. 68 for how to compile and present your CV.

Dear Sirs,

I have just read the article 'Who's the new girl sitting in my seat?' in the 26 January 1990 edition of the *Daily Telegraph*. I found it very interesting and wonder if you can help me.

I am returning to the UK later this year (I will be living in Hertfordshire), having spent six years abroad because of my husband's employment.

For the first year in-country I was not employed. The opportunity then arose for me to be employed as a secretary to my husband – not an ideal working situation but it has been quite successful. However I do feel that it has been somewhat claustrophobic, and I was very limited in the scope of my function due to our geographical location. Therefore my skills have not been utilized to the full and I may have fallen behind my UK counterparts.

(a)   would you consider me a candidate for one of your courses?

(b)   at age fifty-five what chance would I have of employment in the UK?

I enclose an up-to-date CV for your perusal. Whilst being very happy in a secretarial role I would like to widen my scope. Therefore I would not necessarily be looking for a secretarial position, and would be open to other suggestions.

I look forward to hearing from you in due course.

Yours faithfully

Mrs C. Anderson

Dear Madam,

I am writing to you for information about the kind of courses I read about in the article on the Features Page of last week's *Daily Telegraph* which gave the address of your organization.

As you can see I am working abroad – having returned to the teaching profession after a gap of about ten years. (My ex-husband did not want me working in Oman with him, and even when I was in the UK arranging the divorce he took steps to prevent me returning to Oman to teach until he had himself left the country in 1987.) To fit myself for this level of teaching after many years away I did an M.Phil. course in Education at Southampton University while waiting for the divorce to come through, but while I like Oman, I do not feel 'stretched' in this post and also (now I have reached the age of fifty) miss being in England with children and family.

I should like to learn what, if anything, I can do here to enrol for any suitable course to get me into the business world or administration as I do not want to wait till I return to the UK, on leave, in mid-June till I begin finding out more about your courses. Do you, for example, run any in the Manchester area where I have a house? And are there any courses there during late June or July?

Whatever information you can send me to help steer me on to a path to a more rewarding career would be most appreciated.

Yours sincerely
Jane Parkinson

Dear Sir,

I am a forty-one-year-old female teacher educated to degree standard (chemistry/mathematics), presently job-sharing three days per week at a school in Birmingham. I have recently passed O-levels in business studies, accounts and RSA typing skills at night school. For some time now I have gradually become more and more disillusioned with teaching. I feel that I should make a more concerted effort to leave my profession and find a new and more satisfying career.

At present I require assistance to help me to choose the most suitable occupation. I know that I am particularly interested in management, conservation and the environment. If you can offer any information or guidance on career-changing workshops etc., I would be very grateful.

I look forward to your reply.

Yours sincerely
Mrs A. Griffiths

What do I enjoy doing?

What you do in your spare time is very important. After all, we live our lives for the ability to indulge in pleasurable activities – and believe me, they are not all found at work! Here is a list of leisure activities: tick the items you enjoy or would like to do if you had the time or the opportunity.

	I do this, or would do this	I enjoy this	Rank
Reading			
Writing			
Solving puzzles			
Amateur dramatics			
Listening to music			

Drawing or painting
_____

Collecting things
_____

Visiting friends
_____

Playing sports
_____

Travelling
_____

Camping
_____

Keep fit
_____

Voluntary work
_____

Helping on a
committee
_____

Driving
_____

Gardening
_____

DIY
_____

Playing with my
children
_____

Knitting
_____

Making things
_____

Embroidery
_____

Flower arranging
_____

_____

Other activities

_____

Now look again at the list – what would you like to do more of? As before, rank them in order of importance to you by placing a (1) next to the most important, and so on downwards.

An exercise on your own

Look back now at what you enjoy and what you are good at and complete the following table, picking out the interests and abilities you have chosen as being the most important to you.

What I enjoy	What I am good at
1.	1.
2.	2.
3.	3.

Now you have a summary of your main interests and your strongest abilities. Have a look and decide if there are any that seem to go together. Are there things that you enjoy that you are also good at? If so, perhaps your interests come from what you think you do well. In this case you may wish to choose a job which uses your interests and talents. On the other hand, what you are good at and what you enjoy may be totally different.

For example, Mary enjoyed swimming, playing chess and collecting antiques. Two of these were things she did alone: she enjoyed the freedom of being able to go swimming when she wanted, on her own, without needing to rely on others and collecting antiques was also a very personal hobby. Chess allowed her to do something she liked in a social setting. She balanced these activities with what she was good at – dealing with the public and solving problems, skills she put to good use in her part-time work with the local Citizens' Advice Bureau.

At work, we cannot always do all the things we enjoy as well as those that we are good at. If you can do what you enjoy in your free time, you can leave your work for what you are good at.

What do I want to get out of a job?

Here's a questionnaire that enables you to look at what might be important to you. Tick the column that applies to you. If you get stuck, leave a blank and come back to that section later.

	This describes me	This does not describe me
A. Working with things/ideas		
1. Working with equipment or figures rather than people		
2. I prefer working alone with my ideas rather than with other people		
3. I like to feel secure at work		
4. I like to be left to get on with the job		
B. Working with people		
5. I want to work somewhere I can make friends		
6. I would like to work where I could help others		
7. I would like to get to know customers well		
8. I like to co-operate rather than compete		
C. Recognition		
9. I would like to gain personal acclaim for my work		
10. I like to tell others about what I do or would do at work		
11. I like to be the centre of attention or in the public eye		
12. I like people to notice what I've done		
D. Bearing		
13. I would enjoy a job where I would have to talk, persuade or advise people		
14. I like making decisions at work		

	This describes me	This does not describe me
15. I would be happy to control others and supervise		
16. I like to contribute my ideas and sometimes change how things are done		

E.   Using knowledge

17. I like to look information up in books		
18. I would like to be well versed on a particular subject at work and sought out for my advice		
19. I like to find out facts		
20. I like doing jobs where I can get down and concentrate for a period		

F.   Artistic

21. I like using my artistic ability		
22. I need to work in pleasant surroundings		
23. I like to draw and make things or play a musical instrument		
24. I like to design and plan out what I'm doing		

G.   Getting on

25. I like control over the way I do things		
26. I like to win in situations at work		
27. I like to see a career structure in the company I work for		
28. I want to get promoted and maybe get to the top		

Summary

The seven types of need from the questionnaire you have just done are summarized below. Which was the most important to you? There were four questions in each section. Where was your highest score and why?

	List in order of importance to you
A. Working with things	
B. Working with people	
C. Recognition	
D. Bearing	
E. Using knowledge	
F. Artistic	
G. Getting on	
H. What else might be important to you at work?	

Linking enjoyment, skills and needs

Having worked through these exercises which looked at what you enjoy, what you are good at and what you need, complete the following table.

What I enjoy	What I am good at	What I need
1.	1.	1.
2.	2.	2.
3.	3.	3.

Can you see any similarities? Can you make out any links? It would probably be useful for you to discuss your answers with someone else.

> Make notes here and share your thoughts. What does this tell you about you?

What changes would you like to make?

An example

Let's have a look at one of these questionnaires, completed by Susan. Her answers looked like this:

What I enjoy	What I am good at	What I need
1. Reading	1. Verbal and written	1. Working with people
2. Visiting friends	2. Memory	2. Using knowledge
3. Observation	3. Flower arrangement	3. Recognition

Background on Susan

Susan is married, with two children of six and nine. Now the children are at school, she'd like to return to work part-time. Although the school holidays are difficult, her husband does shift work and could arrange his shifts to cover most of the time she is at work.

Susan has four O-levels – English, maths, geography and needlework. She has not worked for nine and a half years, since she gave up a clerical post in accounts with a large company to have her first child. She is now forty-one and feeling bored while her children are at school.

What she's doing now

After completing the questionnaires, Susan felt that working in a library would not only fit her answers but was one of the things she'd always been interested in doing. There were no jobs advertised locally so she wrote a letter to the head librarian, sending her CV. There were still no jobs available, so Susan offered her services voluntarily when the library was moving a section to another part of the building.

This got Susan a job as soon as one was available. She so endeared herself to the library staff that, as soon as a post became free, they organized it so it could be part-time to fit Susan's family commitments.

Since taking the post, Susan has benefited from training offered by the local authority and will be applying for the next supervisory post that is available.

Notes on Chapter 2

3 Looking to the Future

Harnessing the power of your imagination

Chapter 2 aimed to let you learn some things about yourself and to discover what kind of area you might feel happiest and most fulfilled working in. But getting a job after years spent bringing up a family isn't necessarily an end in itself. For many women, it's all part of changing their lives and pointing them in the direction they want to go in – of being in charge of their own destiny. The whole business therefore needs to be seen in the broader framework of how you envisage your future.

Focusing on priorities

Once you have decided you want to change your life, you need to sort out what is most important to you. Here's a tough but effective way of honing in on the most meaningful elements of your life. Imagine that you only have five years left to live. Write down a list of five things that you would want to achieve in that time.

1.
2.
3.
4.
5.

Now imagine that you only have one year to live. Write down five things you would like to do in that one year.

> 1.
>
> 2.
>
> 3.
>
> 4.
>
> 5.

Now imagine you have just one month to live. Write down a list of the people whom you would want to be with.

> 1.
>
> 2.
>
> 3.
>
> 4.
>
> 5.

Now imagine you have just twenty-four hours left. Write down five things you would do in that time.

> 1.
>
> 2.
>
> 3.
>
> 4.
>
> 5.

And finally, one minute left. What would you do in that time?

>

Cross through any negative images that come up, and look at the positive ones.

If you have decided that you want to change things in your life, first you must be able to imagine what your life would be like if it were different. The key is to start with something simple; 95 per cent of the decisions you make are unconscious – for example, when you drive a car you never really think about putting it into first or second gear. You are more likely to be thinking about other things while you are driving along, like what you are going to do when you reach your destination.

Our unconscious plans are often the ones that come to fruition. However, this part of the book is about creating conscious plans. If you have been really enthusiastic about something and then gone home and thought about it, one of two things usually happens. Either you put some flesh on the bones of your idea and your plan really takes off, or you begin to think of all the reasons why it won't work after all.

Dreaming – the first step to achieving

This is a key to help you create what you want in your life. If you're not the kind of person who is used to daydreaming, try a simple one first. Imagine yourself on holiday; think about where you would be, what you would be doing, the kind of food and drink you'd be eating and enjoying. Dreaming is about using the information that you already know.

Let's pause for a moment, while I ask you to imagine the smell of newly baked bread or freshly percolated coffee. The point of using your imagination and dreaming is that, once you have an outline of the dream, you can then begin to think about it more and more in detail until you can bring it back into your own reality.

One good way of starting the dreaming process is to give yourself a physical check-up. Think about each part of your body:

Feet	Are they cool or are they sticky?
Legs	Are they heavy or light?
Tummy	Do you feel hungry or full?
Back	Do you need a firm back massage?
Arms	Do they ache?
Face	Would it enjoy a warm/cool flannel?
Hair	Does it need a comb?

Try to do some things such as taking a shower or having a snack, that will make you feel warm and comfortable and relaxed. Then begin your dream, one step at a time. We all have problems and we all have aches and pains. Try and concentrate on those parts of your body that do feel comfortable.

I don't pretend that this will be easy, because the power of your negative thoughts about what you can't achieve will be very strong. You need to counteract it with as many positive thoughts about yourself as possible.

Imagining and dreaming are very powerful processes. Some successful athletes spend 75 per cent of their time visualizing themselves achieving the results they need. The other 25 per cent of their time is spent training.

Once you have formulated your idea of what you want to see in the future, then you need to focus on how you can get there.

Visions of the future

First make sure you are relaxed (if you have difficulty doing this, see p. 44). Sit or lie in a comfortable position, read through the exercise and then follow these steps.

Close your eyes and imagine yourself somewhere in five years' time. Your life has been incredibly successful, and you've got out of it exactly what you wanted for your highest good. Now try to set the scene:

- Where are you in the world?
- Who are you with?
- Are you working. If so where? And doing what?
- What sort of home do you live in?
- Who is there with you?
- What are they doing?
- What are you wearing?
- What are the expressions on the other people's faces?

If you can imagine your goal, where you want to be in five years' time, then you are already part of the way there. It is not easy to visualize the future, so for one week try the exercise every morning when you wake up and every evening before you go to bed. Each time try to build up a more detailed picture. Don't worry if the picture is very fuzzy to begin with. It would be a miracle if you could have a clear picture of the total future (in fact if you could do that for yourself or anyone else you could probably make lots of money as a clairvoyant). Generally the picture will take about three weeks to build. Keep trying, and every time you think of your day focus your thoughts more tightly around the questions.

Once you begin to get a clear picture of what you would like, you then need to 'place' that image inside your unconscious. 'Placing' your image means putting it in your memory so that you can use it again. For example, a familiar jingle will place in your mind a particular TV commercial. There are emotional 'placemats' as well –

for example, couples often have 'our song'. Another 'placemat' might be the word 'school'. What does that word conjure up for you?

Learning to relax

If you are still having problems with your visualization of a successful future, let's try one more exercise. It will help if you lie down and have some very soft music playing. Try this exercise with a partner. Get them to read this exercise whilst you try to imagine what they are saying.

Partner reads . . .

While you are lying there concentrate on your breathing. Feel the warm air as you breathe out and the cooler air as you breathe in.

- As you breathe in, say to yourself 'relaxation'.
- As you breathe out, imagine the breath passing through any part of your body that feels stiff or aches.
- Now take your concentration down to your feet. Screw up your toes and then flex them out. Screw them up again and flex them out and let your feet drop to the side.
- Now take your concentration to your calves. Tense them and relax, tense again and relax.
- Now think about your knees. Tense them and relax, tense again and relax.
- Now take your concentration to your thighs. Tense them and relax, tense again and relax.
- Now think about your buttocks. Squeeze them together and on an outward breath let them go. Squeeze them together again and on an outward breath let them go again.
- Now tense the whole of your right leg and then let it go. Now tense the whole of your left leg and let it go.
- Now take your concentration to your hands, make fists and squeeze them together and then let them go.
- Think about your arms. Lift them from the elbows, and them drop them down to the floor.
- Now think about your shoulders. Scrunch them up towards your ears and on an outward breath let them go.
- Think about your tummy muscles. On an inward breath pull them in tight. On an outward breath just let them go.

- Now turn your attention to your face. Screw your eyes up tight and on an outward breath relax. Screw your nose up tight and on an outward breath relax. Now clench your jaw tight, then on an outward breath let it flop open. Make sure that your lips are slightly parted and that your jaw is relaxed.

Now that you feel more relaxed try an exercise using your imagination. Ask a friend to read it slowly and quietly, leaving about ten seconds between each sentence. If you do not have a friend handy, why not dictate the exercise on to a cassette tape and play it to yourself. The whole exercise should take about ten to fifteen minutes – leave lots of time for the 'imagining' part. Imagine you are lying in the sunshine on a warm beach in Tahiti. Imagine that you can hear the waves gently lapping on to the soft sand. Imagine that you can see the yellow glow of the warm sun through your closed eyes. Imagine you feel yourself bathed in warmth and sunlight. Now imagine that you open your eyes and you can see a bird flying through the sky. Imagine the colour of that bird and imagine it gracefully flying. Now imagine your bird landing somewhere – think about where and what it is doing. Now imagine it flying away into the distance and think about where it is going.

Now slowly breathe in and out and imagine the scene that might be in the backdrop. Imagine the colours. What do the people look like?

Now concentrate again on your breathing. Feel the cool air that you breathe in and the warmer air that you breathe out. Breathe like this for the next two minutes.

Now being to flex your feet. Put some movement into your hands and arms, roll gently over on to one side, and take another little rest before you finally get up and stretch.

Past successes

Here is yet another idea to help if you are having problems in getting your vision of the future right. Let's have a look back and see how successful you have been in the past.

Divide your life into five equal or near-equal segments – for example, if you are thirty-five each segment would be seven years long, ages 0–7 being the first segment.

- For each time segment look at three successful things that you achieved. Each time segment will then add up to fifteen successes in your life. Don't be afraid to write more in each segment if you can.

- Now circle your top ten successes.
- Think back to each different success. See if you can conjure up a picture of you being successful – what were the events, what were your thoughts and feelings, and what were you doing at the time?

By placing this successful scene in your mind you will automatically begin to recall the things you enjoyed about that section of your life. As you recall that successful scene, whenever something comes up that you enjoyed jot it down on the sheet entitled 'I would like more of this!'

I would like more of this!

Success chart

For each period pick at least three greatest successes. Here are some of mine.

Years	Successes
0–7	Learning to read
	Making first childhood friend
	Learning to ride a bike
8–14	Getting into grammar school
	Winning road safety award
	Learning to swim
15–21	Becoming a woman
	Passing driving test
	Being promoted into boss's job
	Not marrying the first man who asked
22–28	Learning about training
	Making new friends
	Escaping from home
	Rebuilding a cottage
	Passing IPM (personnel qualification)
29–35	Having a baby
	Rebuilding a house
	Getting a job after having a baby
	Sailing across the Channel

When you do your own, pick out the ten you like best.

Your personal success chart

Adjust column 1 as necessary if you are older than thirty-five, or choose different segments of your own, e.g. ten years.

Years	Successes
0–7	
8–14	
15–21	
22–28	
29–35	

Setting objectives

Dreaming of the future and rediscovering the feeling of past successes should have helped you work out some goals for yourself – what we will call a 'success image'. But don't get muddled between goals and objectives. It is all very well having a goal, but goals are long-term and not always achievable; only objectives are truly achievable. Many people who try to set themselves goals and call them objectives think they have failed when they don't reach them. A goal describes the long-term direction in which you are heading – for example, 'to own my own house'; an objective can be reached more quickly. But if you achieve your objectives on the way, you stand a much better chance of making it to your ultimate goal.

Objectives must be measurable

There are certain rules for setting objectives. First of all, they must be 'measurable' – e.g. 'To earn £10,000 a year', not just 'To earn good money'.

Objectives must be specific

Objectives should not be too general, indeed they should be as specific as possible, e.g. not 'Everybody should like me', but that 'John should greet me on arrival at work'.

Objectives must be desirable

You should place your objectives on a 1–10 rating scale for desirability, so you know which ones to concentrate on and which are most important to you. If you rate the difficulty or effort needed to achieve those objectives, it will help you to avoid choosing all the most difficult ones in the first week. Some of them will be easily achievable, e.g. finish the ironing by lunchtime, but some will be more difficult, e.g. finish the five-mile fun run! This objective would need lots of other objectives *en route* to help you achieve it, e.g.

- Visit the gym twice every week
- Adopt a more sensible diet
- Go running every day

Now think about your shorter-term objectives and your general long-term goal:

Objectives must be reasonable

Finally, objectives need to be reasonable. If they can't be accomplished in about six weeks, set yourself some smaller sub-objectives that you can complete today or within a week, just like on the five-mile run example.

Linking objectives to your success image – the five-year plan

If you are going to change your life, you need to attach your objectives to your success image.

Let's now imagine that success image again. If you were to achieve your goal in five years' time, what would you have to be doing in four years' time to get there? Then take a journey back in time three years, two years and one year, to get to your success image.

My goal in five years' time would be

To achieve this in four years' time I would be doing

In three years' time I would be doing

In two years' time I would be doing

In one year's time I would be doing

At each stage you move backwards through time and ask your unconscious mind to help you see a picture of yourself being highly successful on your way to completion of your objectives.

When you have this picture in your mind, decide how good it is. Where would you place it on a score card of 1–100? How would you need to change this image in your mind to score 100? Now make the changes to your success image and to your plan for the next five years. To help you complete this plan, try to draw a picture that you will associate with your goal. It doesn't need any artistic pretensions – it just needs to be a picture that you can lodge in your mind as a reminder to you of your aims.

Draw your picture here. Use colour if it helps.

Step-by-step short-term objectives – building up the picture

Now that you have a goal and some objectives for the next five years, let's concentrate on some more specific objectives for the next year. Five things to achieve may well seem a lot, but for encouragement read on to see what objectives other women have set themselves.

3 months

1.

2.

3.

4.

5.

6 months

1.

2.

3.

4.

5.

1 year

1.

2.

3.

4.

5.

Here are some examples of the kind of objectives you might set yourself.

---

3 months
1. Send off five job applications per week and prepare my CV (see Chapter 4).

2. Cut down to ten cigarettes per day.

3. Take up walking to the shops or school.

4. Visit my ageing aunt.

5. Find out what adult education classes are offered locally.

6 months
1. Plan a holiday.

2. Organize one whole hour just for myself every weekend.

3. Change my image – different hairstyle, younger clothes, stop smoking.

4. Visit my closest friends.

5. Find out how to get promoted at work.

1 year
1. Change the family's diet to low-fat and more healthy eating.

2. Save up for a holiday.

3. Buy a small car.

4. Take a more active role at my children's school.

5. Take up a hobby just for me.

Now look at some even shorter-term actions you can take to lead you to your longer-term goals.

	What needs to be done	When I shall do it	Measures of success and rewards (see p. 96)
Today			
1.			
2.			
3.			
4.			
5.			
Next week			
1.			
2.			
3.			
4.			
5.			
2 weeks			
1.			
2.			
3.			
4.			
5.			
1 month			
1.			
2.			
3.			
4.			
5.			

	What needs to be done	When I shall do it	Measures of success and rewards (see p. 96)

3 months

1.

2.

3.

4.

5.

6 months

1.

2.

3.

4.

5.

1 year

1.

2.

3.

4.

5.

Notes on Chapter 3

4 Going Back to Work

Now that you've thought long and hard about goals and objectives, let's get back to the nitty-gritty of finding and getting a job. If you are going to work for somebody else, then you'll need to prepare a record of your abilities and experience. This is often called a curriculum vitae, or CV for short. There's a form on pp. 68–71 that gives a list of the main things that you'll need to cover when preparing one.

You could have had a gap of many years since you worked. Many women wait until there is a milestone in their child's (or youngest child's) development, such as:

- Straight after the baby is born
- When the baby is off the breast
- When the child starts playschool
- When the child starts nursery school
- When the child starts junior school
- When the child starts secondary school
- When the child leaves school and goes to work
- When the child goes off to university or leaves home
- (add your own)

Other reasons for returning after a long period away include:

- When the woman feels that she is not being stretched enough mentally at home
- When she feels bored
- When there has been trauma in her life, e.g. divorce or the death of a family member

- When she has been a carer in the family and she can no longer fulfil this role or it is no longer needed

During the time that you've been away from work you have certainly not been 'not working' – you have undertaken a whole host of activities which happen to have been unpaid.

What can you do that's of interest to an employer?

Running a household successfully involves many of the basic management and administrative skills; these and other personal skills that are equally useful in the workplace were discussed in Chapter 2. Here are some further areas in which you may well have experience and that would stand you in good stead with a prospective employer.

Attending adult education classes

What did you learn? Was it relevant in any way to work? Even if it was a leisure activity and bears no relevance to the particular job you are applying for, it will at least show that you have the ability to concentrate and study.

British Red Cross or St John's Ambulance

Many employers require a member of their staff to be a first aider.

Choir

Are you a good team member, a sociable person? Did you use organizing skills? Have you contributed in any way with ideas or actions?

Community Organization

There are many roles that you may have played or tasks that you may have undertaken that would be of interest to an employer.

Parent-teacher association

Have you learnt negotiating skills by dealing with the local authority or with teachers?

Sports team

Have you the drive to win and succeed?

Musical group

Are you able to concentrate? Are you tenacious when learning a piece?

Tenants' association

Have you learnt to lobby or discuss/implement plans?

Voluntary work

Have you had to raise money and implement plans?

Scouting/guiding, youth club leader, or YMCA/YWCA

Have you had experience working with young people and becoming a mentor/coach?

Photographic club

Are you artistic?

Quiz team

Are your reactions fast?

Church activities

Other organization

All employers will try to use your skills. What are yours?

The list is endless – but every activity you may have undertaken whilst at home will offer an employer some benefit. Here is an example of how you would put these skills into practice in a job application or interview.

Achievements to parade to an employer

These are the sort of achievements and skills that you may have under your belt from being a member of such social groups:

- Elected as an officer in a club, e.g. chairman, secretary.
  If you are, what do you do?
- Managed or coached an amateur team.
  What were your responsibilities and achievements?
- Gained any award or honour.
  How hard did you have to work for it?
- Learned another language.
  Can this be used at work? The arrival of the Single European Market in 1992 is bringing more opportunity to use foreign languages at work.
- Organized an extension to be built on your house.
  Did you design the plans? Did you set up and supervise the builders?
- Helped prevent a disaster.
  Are you observant? Do you notice when things are not right?
- Helped someone who was injured.
  Would you make a good first-aider at work? Are you calm in a crisis?
- Won a sports trophy.
  What did you have to do? What skills were involved?
- Had letters published in a newspaper, or written an article or even a book.
  Have you got any ambition to write creatively?
- Been involved in amateur dramatics.
  Can you remember lines? Give direction? Organize costumes or sets? Sell tickets? Arrange publicity?
- Gained a certificate for adult education.
  Have you the ability to learn?
- Passed an advanced driving test.
  Are you a careful driver?
- Completed a marathon/other sport.

Have you got the ability, determination to finish and the drive to keep going?
- Gained a life-saving certificate for swimming.

There may be other achievements that you are proud of that are not listed here. Please list them now.

1.	
2.	
3.	
4.	
5.	
6.	
7.	
8.	
9.	

Where to look for a job

If you are looking for a job, where do you start? 'Advertisements', might seem the obvious answer; however, 70 per cent of the jobs that are actually on offer are never actually advertised. So how do you get a chance at these?

Ask around

Let everybody you know have the details of the kind of employment that you might be looking for. You'll be surprised who has got a friend or an uncle who knows somebody who knows somebody else who is looking for a person like you!

Go for it

Why not compile a list of those companies within travelling distance of your home that might be offering the type of thing that you're looking for? It certainly won't hurt to write to them or telephone to ask if they have any vacancies.

Newspapers

The first paper to look in is of course your own local paper. Most areas have a number of these – the freesheets that will come through your letterbox as well as the ones that you can buy in a newsagent. When you are looking seriously, buy the ones for areas adjacent to your own as well, as employers cannot always afford to advertise in more than one.

The newspapers to look in are:

- *Guardian*
- *Times*
- *Independent*
- *Daily Telegraph*
- *Sunday Times*
- *Observer*

Certain papers specialize in particular career areas on different days of the week.

Guardian

One of the best days to buy the *Guardian* is Saturday, where all the job advertisements published during the week preceding appear again, all together, in the 'Weekend' section.

On Mondays you will find jobs advertising secretarial posts, jobs in marketing and a very large section on the media, creative professions and the arts.

Tuesdays are dedicated to jobs in education.

Public appointments – the Civil Service, nationalized industries and local government – are advertised on Wednesdays.

Thursday's edition contains a mixture of jobs in science, computing, technology, and the financial and business sectors.

On Fridays the appointments relate to jobs connected with the environment.

Times

The *Times*, like the *Guardian*, has different days for different types of jobs. Every day it carries secretarial appointments.

Mondays concentrate on education.

Tuesday's edition offers jobs in the public sector and the legal profession.

Wednesdays are for jobs in the media.

Thursdays are for more general appointments and those in banking, accountancy, engineering and management.

Independent

Mondays are good days to look for jobs in science, engineering and technology.

On Tuesdays it is mainly jobs in accountancy and general management.

Wednesday is media day.

Thursdays cover private sector, education and appointments for graduates.

Friday looks at jobs in the legal profession.

Daily Telegraph

The *Daily Telegraph* appointments page always appears on Thursdays. Advertisements here are for jobs in personnel and training, selling and management, as well as technical and professional.

Sunday Times and Observer

Most of the posts advertised here are very senior.

Specialist magazines

Most career disciplines have specialist magazines associated with them. If you are not sure where to look, go to your local reference library and ask for a copy of *BRAD* (*British Rate and Data*), which lists every publication and its advertising rates. It will indicate the magazines that sell employment vacancy advertising space. You can then look for jobs in those publications at the library.

Agencies

There are two types of agencies where you would find a job. The government agency is called a Job Centre. Jobs here are advertised on a self-service rack. Make a note of the job number that you are interested in and take it along to the clerk at the desk. He or she will then telephone and make an appointment for you for an interview.

While you are there, register for a free copy of *Executive Post*, which will be sent to your home. This newspaper contains many helpful hints on job seeking as well as lots of varied and interesting job vacancies.

Private agencies generally specialize in clerical and secretarial work and may want to test your speeds, so be prepared for this. There are also specialized agencies that deal with nursing, catering and more manual occupations. Here you will not get a test, but they will often want to see proof of any qualifications that you may have. Agencies will be listed in your local Thomson Directory or the Yellow Pages. In addition, some libraries will be happy to help you with a list of local agencies or specialist agencies, for example those agencies which deal with computer personnel in London or major cities.

A word of advice

Find out as much as you can about a job before you apply for it, and certainly before you have an interview. This will avoid wasting everybody's time if the job, the candidate or the company are unsuitable for each other. See p. 128 for further assistance on this point.

Applying for a job

When you've seen a job advertisement that appeals to you, you will need to write a covering letter to send with your CV (*see* 'Compiling Your CV', pp. 68–73). The letter should be no longer than one side of A4, and should cover the points raised in the advertisement concisely. Your prospective employer can read the details of your past work experience in your CV. Over the page is a sample advertisement and reply.

Small legal practice seeks reliable receptionist/
secretary. Your duties would include operating
Monarch switchboard, typing and other general
office duties. Salary £9,500–£11,000, according
to age and experience.

Apply to Alan Smith
Smith and Frye Associates
101 High Street
Milton Keynes

Karen Thomas
45 Mildenhall Road
Milton Keynes, Bucks.

Alan Smith
Smith and Frye Associates
101 High Street
Milton Keynes, Bucks.

27th September 1991

Dear Mr Smith,

In response to your advertisement in the *Bedfordshire
Reporter*, I am writing to apply for the post of secretary/
receptionist. Before having my first child four years ago, I
worked for several years as a secretary at the head office of
Sainsbury's in Canterbury, and a further year as a personal
assistant for Kent County Council. My typing speed is 55
wpm, and I am capable of operating a switchboard. I enjoy
working as part of a team, and after four years looking after my
two sons I am eager to return to working outside home. I feel I
would fit in well as part of your company, and look forward to
hearing from you.

Yours sincerely,

Karen Thomas

The letter should explain that you have the right qualifications, and say that you are willing to learn those you don't have: you may be a competent typist, for example, but need a few hours to learn how to use a word processor. Don't be negative or apologetic – remember you're selling yourself, and should highlight your good points.

If you don't find any of the jobs you've seen advertised appealing, it may well be worth writing to a company that you are interested in working for, but which has no vacancies that you know of. Companies often recruit staff from speculative letters they have kept on file, and your letter may arrive just at the right moment. It is best to phone the company before you write to find out the name of the person you should write to. It is more likely that a letter to 'Anna Payne' will get a response than one simply to 'the personnel manager'. Here is an example of a letter to a large clothes store:

Rachel McArthur
22 Colenso Road
Manchester

Anna Payne
Personnel Manager
Prentice's Department Store
High Street, Manchester

30th February 1991

Dear Anna Payne,

After six years looking after my three children, I would like to return to work. Ideally I would like to work part-time, and have written to you as in the last few years I have seen part-time posts advertised at Prentice's. My work experience includes one year as an accounts clerk, and two years as a shop assistant in a women's clothes shop. I was promoted to assistant manageress in the clothes shop, and worked a further eight months before leaving to have my first child. I would be happy to work either on the sales side, or in the accounts office; perhaps I could come in and discuss any possibilities with you? If that is not convenient, I would be grateful if you could keep my details on file. Many thanks.

Yours sincerely,
Rachel McArthur

Compiling your CV

Your CV, or curriculum vitae, is a record of your experiences and achievements. Nowadays almost all employers require one before they will call you for interview.

- They use it to eliminate those candidates they feel are totally unsuitable.
- They use it to help prepare themselves for the interview – i.e. to get to know you a bit before you arrive and work out the questions they are going to ask you.
- They keep it on file in case other suitable vacancies arise.
- They pass it to other managers or other parts of the organization who may have a suitable vacancy for you.

Your CV is your ambassador, and must represent you well when you try to get a job. Here's an example of the kind of format to follow. The information in *italics* is for your guidance only. Everything else should actually appear on the CV that you send off. A CV always looks better presented, and is easier for the prospective employer to read, if it is typed. If you can't type or don't own a typewriter, ask your friends.

Curriculum Vitae

Personal details

Name: (*include your title: Mrs/Miss/Ms or Mr*)

Date of Birth: } (*only give*
Marital Status: } *these if you wish*)

Address: _____

_____

Postcode: _____   General Health: _____
(*Write your comments*)

Telephone Number   Daytime: _____

Evening: _____

Work experience
(*Most recent first, but do not mention part-time fill-in posts such as cleaner or bar person if they are not now relevant to what you are looking for. When completing the section entitled duties and*

responsibilities write what you did each day/what you achieved at work each month/year.)

Title of job	Dates to–from	Duties and responsibilities

Training

(Leave out any headings that do not apply to you, but remember the courses you may have been on whilst at home, e.g. French for Beginners, Cake Decoration or English O-level.)

TRAINING AT WORK
(Given on-the-job. What were you trained to do at work?)

Skills Achieved	Dates

COURSES AT WORK

Course Title	Dates

LEISURE COURSES

Course Title	Dates

Secondary education

Dates	Name and Address of School	Achievements or subjects studied/examinations passed
Dates	Name of College/University	Achievements/subjects studied/ examinations passed

Spare-time activities

(See previous list for ideas of skills you may have that would be of interest to an employer.)

Additional information

Have you got a driving licence?
Can you speak a foreign language?
What can you say about your own character?

Are you hard-working/reliable/punctual?
Are you able to communicate well with people?
Are you accurate?
Are you clear on the telephone?
Are you a problem-solver?
Are you able to respond quickly?
Do you enjoy a challenge?
Are you able to prioritize?
Can you work on your own?
Do you work well in a team?
Are you used to handling money?
Are you able to delegate work?
Are you able to sell ideas?
Are you able to manage other people?

Think about what the employer is looking for. There will be many clues in the advertisement. If they want someone to work on their own initiative, don't be afraid to tell them in your application that you can do that. If you don't sell yourself you can be certain that no one else will! Your application will be even better supported if you can give examples of when you've had to work on your own, as when decorating your new house or when preparing the accounts of a small business whilst at home with your children.

References (see p. 73)

Personal skills

To help you in compiling your CV here's a list of the sort of personal skills that companies look for:

Administration	Operating equipment
Advising people	Organizing people and work
Answering enquiries	Persuading people
Arranging functions/events	Planning work
Analyzing	Programming computers
Checking for accuracy	Promoting events
Co-ordinating people/events	Raising funds
Communicating	Recording data
Controlling budgets	Repairing mechanical
Counselling people	equipment
Delegating tasks	Representing an
Drawing charts/diagrams	organization
Editing documents	Reviewing current business
Figure work	literature
Filing	Running meetings
Giving information	Selling products/services
Handling customer	Serving the public
complaints	Setting agendas
Innovating	Setting up demonstrations
Inspecting manufactured	Speaking in public
goods	Staff management
Interpreting data	Supervising staff
Interviewing people	Teaching
Maintaining records	Telephone answering skills
Mentoring	Telephone sales skills
Monitoring	Training staff
Motivating people	Writing letters/reports
Negotiating	

Remember also that companies are interested in your leisure activities, because these may tell them something about you, in particular in relation to the job in question. For example, if someone gave as their hobbies on their CV only reading and chess, and they were applying to you for a job where they would be working with the public, might you not have doubts about that person? When applying for a job, make sure you emphasize the interests and leisure activities that an employer would find relevant.

Leisure activities that you might like to put on your CV

Boating or sailing
Birdwatching
Building models
Climbing
Collecting stamps/coins
Cookery
Cycling
Dancing
DIY
Drawing
Dressmaking/knitting
Electronic projects
Fishing
Gardening
Keeping tropical fish
Keeping pets
Keeping fit
Maintaining your car
Painting
Photography
Playing word games/doing
  crosswords
Playing musical
  instrument/s

Playing darts
Poetry
Pottery
Reading
Swimming
Using a home computer
Voluntary work
Watching/playing sport
Winemaking/brewing beer
Walking
Writing
Any additional sports or
  hobbies:

_____

_____

_____

_____

_____

_____

References

You will probably be asked to give the name of one or two people who will provide references, even if you don't actually do this on your CV. Employers generally want you to give the name of your last employer. But what if your last job was as a cleaner or temporary postman, just because it fitted your circumstances – say to work within school hours? Leave out that employer as a reference if it is not relevant, and go back to your last relevant employer.

'What about if it was ten years ago?' you may ask. Well, still quote them. Most employers keep long-term records.

'What about if the company no longer exists?' Again, you can still quote them if you wish – it's the employer's job to track them down if they want a reference.

Alternatively, quote someone else in a position of authority who can speak about you. Women who have attended the Dow-Stoker Returner courses can always give the course tutor as a referee. This is sometimes possible, too, if you have attended a further or adult education college. Don't be afraid to ask the tutor if he or she would be willing to give you a reference. Other useful people may be the secretary of a committee you've served on or someone you've done temporary work for.

If you get really stuck there's always your minister or doctor, but try to make the reference as 'work-specific' as you possibly can.

Now complete your own CV

CURRICULUM VITAE

Personal Details

Address:

Name:

Date of Birth:

Marital Status:

General Health:

Telephone Number   Daytime:
                    Evening:

Work experience

Title of Job	Dates to–from	Experience Gained

Training
TRAINING AT WORK

Skills Achieved	Dates

COURSES AT WORK
Course Title   Dates

LEISURE COURSES
Course Title   Dates

Education

Dates   Name and Address of School   Achievements
                 or College

Spare-time activities

Additional information

References

1.   2.

Preparing for an interview

When you're preparing for the interview make sure that you test yourself and have good answers to basic questions like:

- Why am I interested in working for this company?
- What attracted me to the job/career advertised?
- What sort of things can I do or learn that will be needed at work? A company requiring someone with organizing skills might ask you what skills you'll be bringing to the job. Your answer needs to be something like, 'I know I'm an efficient organizer of events and people. For example, recently I organized a fete at my child's school. This involved co-ordinating all the various stalls, publicizing the event, accounting for the money and persuading numerous people to become volunteers.'

Looking at the interview now in greater detail, here is a questionnaire to use both before and after an interview. Before, it gives you quite a few clues to what you may be asked and will help you to present yourself properly and to prepare your answers. Remember, too, that an interview works both ways – you can also 'interview' the interviewer. If, for instance, no one mentions what the pay will be, it is up to you to ask that question and obtain a satisfactory answer. After an interview, the questionnaire is a good guide to how you did and to what, if anything, went wrong.

Interview review

NAME OF ORGANIZATION: _____

Place of interview: Date: _____

	Good/Bad	Comments
1. Punctual – checked timing of journey beforehand.		
2. My dress – I looked like the other people employed in the job I applied for.		
3. I shook hands and smiled on meeting the interviewer.		

4. I listened well to the meaning
    of the questions during the
    interview.

5. I sat in an open posture and
    avoided nervous mannerisms
    (i.e. not with arms folded).

6. I answered questions fully,
    not just yes/no.

7. I didn't undersell myself.

8. I described my:
    Qualifications
    Previous experience
    Personal interests

9. I pointed out my special
    strengths.

10. I explained why I was suited
    to this job.

11. I described how previous
    experience gave me the skills
    needed for the post.

12. I looked at interviewer whilst
    we were talking.

13. I smiled occasionally.

14. I offered my thanks to the
    interviewer for seeing me and
    shook his/her hand at the
    end.

15. I know the 'next steps', i.e.
    when I will be contacted and
    when I might have to return
    for a second interview.

16. I know the pay and all the
    conditions of employment.

17. I know the start date for the
    post.

Answers I need to improve upon before my next interview

	Next time I'd say
(a) About my last job	
(b) Questions concerning previous jobs	
(c) Dates given in my CV	
(d) Reasons for leaving	
(e) Health	
(f) My personal circumstances	
(g) My future plans or ambitions	
(h) My family circumstances	

Questions to ask the interviewer

I asked about/was given information about:

Pay
Hours
Holidays
Conditions of service
Maternity leave
Career breaks
Staff benefits
Promotion prospects
Training at work
Future developments or changes expected in the employer's
    industry/service

Notes on Chapter 4

5 Communication and Assertiveness

The skills of communication are essential at every level and in every situation of our lives. Whether you are dealing with small children or addressing a board meeting, getting information from the man who's repairing your washing machine or closing a big deal with a new customer, you need to be able to put yourself and your message across. Personality plays a large part in this, so let's start there.

Assertiveness is not what it seems

In the home and in the workplace, women are constantly being urged these days to be more assertive. Its effect is clear – you get what you want, what you think is right, rather than falling in with other people's views. But what exactly does 'assertiveness' mean?

- 'It's just you should speak up a bit more.'
- 'You should let people know your point of view.'
- 'You need to present yourself better.'
- 'You should learn to say "No" more often.'

These are all suggestions I've been given, but most of them are too vague for people to do anything with. For example, when should you 'speak up a bit more'? And does it mean talk louder? When is it appropriate to say more or say less?

To answer some of these questions, let's first look at some of the things assertiveness *isn't*.

Aggressiveness

I was angry with my friend
I told my wrath, My wrath did end.

I was angry with my foe:
I told it not, My wrath did grow. *William Blake (1757–1827)*

Many people think that aggressiveness is assertion. Well, it certainly isn't. Aggressiveness is a destructive pattern of behaviour, established by someone after they have been hurt. It can be either a chronic pattern (like a record that plays all the time) or a 'triggered' pattern.

To explain what is meant by a triggered pattern, here's an example. One woman found that when different family members were all demanding different things and her attention at the same time, 'something blows'. She said, 'It acts like a trigger and you react aggressively.'

We nearly all have these triggers. Take a moment to think about what some of yours may be.

Some of my triggers are

-
-
-
-
-
-
-
-
-
-
-
-
-
-
-
-
-
-

People stuck in an aggressive pattern of behaviour often have a very strong desire to win and will do all sorts of things to achieve this. They think they have to win to gain self-esteem, in other words they don't value themselves highly unless they are constantly winning or one up on other people.

I mentioned that the patterns often arise from a 'hurt'. As a result you may have very little or no self-esteem. The hurt itself may have happened a long time ago, and may even be something that you have forgotten all about. But if you don't value or love yourself it is very easy not to love or value other people. If, on the other hand, you have high self-esteem and value yourself, it is very difficult to fall into this type of negative pattern. To get out of this pattern and to become more assertive you need to learn to like and value yourself.

The typical pattern with aggressiveness is that people attack, over-react, blow up and cause resentment. You hear them say things like,

- 'Why can't everyone live their own lives?'
- 'Why must everyone rely on me?'

The fact that they can't look at the real problems makes them attack someone or something else.

One woman described how she experienced an aggressive pattern: 'I found it very difficult to cope with women over me, especially if I thought that they weren't being fair – although I had no problems when dealing with men. I realized what I was doing and decided to have this problem analyzed, and I traced it back to when I was in hospital as a child. I was suffering from diphtheria, most of the adult staff were women, and nobody was explaining what was happening to me. As a result I was having tantrums. The result was that as an adult I was still reacting as a four-year-old child. I have now had to learn to cope with my problem and think before I react, remembering that I am now an adult.'

This woman was able to come to terms with her aggressive pattern by 'unscrambling' it and beginning to understand the roots of the problem. But how do we unscramble our feelings? One solution is what's called 'good-quality listening', and that's dealt with on p. 113.

Compliments

Not accepting compliments is another example of aggressive behaviour. In my early twenties I found that I would become aggressive when I was given a compliment. When I looked back I realized it was because of a hurt from when I was younger – I had protruding teeth and was the only child in my school at the time to wear braces. As a result I was ridiculed by the other children.

This made me feel in later life that I was very unattractive, because I had had so many negative thoughts about my appearance earlier in my life. In one of my first jobs I plastered on the make-up and wore very executive-type suits. I was on the defensive and wore my make-up as a barrier. Later I found out that I had appeared fierce and unapproachable. I found it unbelievable at that time that boys would genuinely want to ask me out and found me attractive.

After some counselling, which enabled me to unscramble my uncomfortable thoughts about myself, I discovered the root of my problem and am now able to cope better with receiving compliments about my appearance.

Anger

Being assertive does not mean that we will never get angry. Anger is legitimate – it can be a good thing to 'let off steam'. Indeed I think it is positively dangerous to hold negative feelings in. The childhood messages that we get from our parents and teachers are things like, 'Good little girls don't get angry' and 'I hope you're being a good girl today'. This can result in women feeling it's wrong to tell people how they feel, especially if they feel angry. Many women never really express any anger.

The best way to let off steam is with people who love you and don't judge you. However, we could hurt the people who love us most if we don't negotiate with them a time and method for letting out anger.

If you have children, you may have experienced them coming home from school and immediately throwing a tantrum in front of you. However, they have come home to a safe place where they know they are loved and that it is safe to have their tantrums. It's often too dangerous to have tantrums at school. We adults do the same: we come home from work and start complaining or picking a fight.

For example, you could be involved in a meeting where the people present are your customers and you cannot show your anger; you gradually get angrier and angrier and store up all your frustrations. A couple of days later you are talking to a close associate and all your anger and frustration surge out as you let go of your feelings about the meeting. Let's hope he or she cares about you enough to say, 'You know you should have called me earlier – you must have been holding this in for days!'

Giving in

Giving in, or submissive behaviour, is more or less the opposite side of the coin to aggressive behaviour. Again it can be chronic or triggered. Many women display the chronic kind and are continuously putting themselves down. The pattern runs like this . . . .

People tend to opt out, criticize themselves, not accept compliments, not make decisions and feel frustrated. One of the typical patterns, when you go back to work or attend a course, is to opt out of this new situation as soon as it gets a little tough, especially if there are domestic problems such as children sick or on holiday.

You may realize that you suffer from this problem, but it is very difficult to break the pattern. You end up not making choices, your life drifts, things happen to you. Rather than you being in control, you lose control.

What happens if you don't make choices? Well, somebody else makes choices for you. Maybe your children will do it or your parents, your partner or your friends, and these choices may not actually be what you wanted.

A woman told how she had spent the last fifteen years of her life 'allowing my husband to make choices for me'. One of these had been that he had suggested going to the Isle of Wight on holiday with the same friends, every year, self-catering. Every summer she ended up doing all the cooking.

She said, 'Every year I end up taking a pair of rubber gloves with me and looking after the children, and every year I end up coming home feeling exhausted. Then I decided I was going to make my own choices from now on. I'd tell my husband I'd rather have a change of holiday and not go with our friends.

'When I told him, his reply was that he thought I had liked going there, and he burst out with, "Thank goodness you told me. I'd love to go abroad – and without our friends!"' The result was that they were both happy and wished they had voiced their opinions many years earlier.

A similar behaviour pattern for women involves not saying what you want and thinking that you are last in the family chain. For instance, if you are cooking chops and one of them is burnt, most women end up eating it themselves. Try taking the best chop next time – but only if you want it!

Saying 'No'

Another example of giving in is not being able to say 'No'. You may be at home when someone calls round and leaves their children with you; you want to do your own thing but don't feel you can say 'No', so you say 'Yes'. Many women have difficulty saying 'No', especially to friends. Sometimes it is slightly easier to say 'No' over the telephone, but face to face many women find it impossible.

Again it is part of the conditioning that women have received in early childhood. It is passed on from generation to generation in a chain, and is very difficult to break.

Let's take an extreme example. For some women, from about 6.30 a.m. to 8.00 a.m. their husband and children are the 'puppeteers', manipulating what they do. Then at work they are at the whim of the boss. Finally, when they get back home once again they are 'in demand', and it is in their nature to work for the family again and put their own wants or needs to the bottom of the pile!

Equality in the home

It is important to remember that everything that has to be done in the home can be shared. If we have sons we should try to change the social pattern and encourage them to help around the house, introducing them to the things that traditionally have been 'women's work'. A lot of mums, however, still lay out their twenty-year-old's washed and ironed clothes on the bed for them each morning and continuously clean up after them, catering for their every need. Women on our courses who have both a boy and girl are now finding daughters rebelling and asking why they have to do everything when their brother does little or nothing. The anomaly is thus brought to the attention of the mother, but mums don't always support the idea of household tasks being fairly divided.

It is frustrating that women are expected to be happy with the traditional women's jobs. If you find these jobs a pleasure then it's OK, but if you don't like them and being 'in service' makes you unhappy you *can* make changes. If a husband has been 'spoilt' by his mother, he can make it very difficult for his wife by comparing them. Swapping jobs at home for a while with your partner may help. Many women resist swapping jobs because they know they could do a job a lot better or quicker themselves, or because they are frightened of 'having a go' at traditional male jobs. You could finish putting up shelves in the kitchen while he does the ironing.

Go on! Have a go – it might be fun!

Hard luck stories

Another typical submissive pattern is for people to cling to their hard luck stories, as well as to put themselves down. They become their own worst enemy and often beat themselves up mentally. 'I'm just a housewife', is a typical put-down. However, if all the jobs a housewife does were put down in a job description people might think twice before saying this. Let's have a look at just a few.

List here all the jobs a housewife does:

-
-
-
-
-
-
-
-
-
-
-
-

How many of these jobs would you like to delegate to someone else? Then why are you still doing them? Write your excuses here!

-

-

-

-

-

-

-

-

-

-

-

-

-

Think about why you have accepted the situation as it is and what you would do if you were totally powerful to change things.

> **Write some ideas here:**
>
> ●
>
> ●
>
> ●
>
> ●
>
> ●
>
> ●

The cause of all this is a common problem in society today – we tend to judge people on their 'professional status', in other words what they do and how much they are paid. This presents a problem for many women, because as a housewife you are not paid.

When we feel lack of status it is easy to cling to our hard luck stories about how totally powerless we are to change the things we'd like to change. Nonsense! If you want to change things, you *can*. Read on!

Things that drive us

Where do you push yourself to put extra energy into things? We have all done tasks where we reward ourselves if we achieve them and 'beat ourselves up' if we don't. Internal 'drivers' are additional pressures that we put on ourselves at work and at home. Many have been identified:

● **Be perfect** – that is, never make a mistake and always be 'good'.

● **Hurry up** – this one is often learnt from our parents. How many times were you told to hurry up, and how many times have you said 'hurry up' to your children? This can turn into a driver where people then feel they have to achieve everything in the fastest possible time. Never mind the quality – watch the speed!

● **I want to please you** – most of us like to be popular and enjoy pleasing other people. However, when this becomes a driver we are often looking for attention when we are doing something. We over-emphasize our needs for other people's approval of what we do. This makes it very difficult for us to be angry with other people or to give criticism.

- **Be strong** – I will achieve all these things in a day even if I am exhausted by the end of it. The driver is that, even though I am suffering, it adds merit to what I do – i.e. I will stand rather than sit, I will struggle through alone rather than ask for help. Many men suffer from this driver; as children they were often told by their parents: 'Be strong! Big boys don't cry', etc.

- **Try hard** – this driver demands that you put extra effort into something, so people try doing things in difficult ways.

You have probably noticed that most of the drivers are at root perfectly normal behaviour. It is when they become 'over-drivers' that problems occur: people concentrate on 'being perfect' to the exclusion of what actually *needs* to be done. Drivers are really about overdoing it.

When we were born we didn't have this difficulty – we did things how we felt like, when we felt like and where we felt like. As very small children, too, we had lots of time to get things done in the same pattern.

Then our parents and teachers started 'managing' us. They wanted us to do better at school (be perfect). They didn't want us to take all day about it (hurry up). They always wanted us to put up with something – for example, I can remember riding in sweltering heat in the back of an old car of my father's, in which the back windows didn't open (be strong). Certainly we had to please people lots of the time – we had to kiss Aunty and show our school report to Uncle to please people. We also had to keep going when we often wanted to give up. I can remember being asked to run the mile at school and my parents encouraging me not to stop (try hard).

However, even knowing all this we still get seduced by the attraction of drivers. All the drivers are exciting, and people who are stuck in this pattern of behaviour often have an incentive to stay in it – they feel that one day they *will* succeed, they *will* finally be perfect, they *will* at last please everyone; they *will* prove that they can get everything done more quickly than everyone else, and they'll *know* that they can undertake anything under the most difficult conditions.

Breaking the mould

If you're stuck in some of these behavioural ruts then you can allow yourself to give it up. You can decide to be imperfect, to do things in your own time, to please yourself, not to be strong and to try only as much as you like.

Manipulation

People who manipulate use guilt and blame – they are powerful weapons to get people to do something. If a relative says something like, 'I haven't heard from you for so long I thought you had emigrated!', what they may really mean is, 'I wish you would come and see me more often.'

This statement may make you angry and have quite the opposite effect from the one they actually want. To punish them, you may leave it even longer before you see them next time. If they were assertive and asked for what they wanted rather than 'manipulated', they would in many cases be more successful.

Some people even resort to emotional blackmail and games, which can end in making everyone unhappy.

Manipulation is just another form of aggressive behaviour. Take the manipulative manager who said to his second-in-command:'Good morning, Clive! Didn't trip over your car in the car park when I arrived at seven this morning.' To show his annoyance, Clive's reaction was to leave his car in the car park that evening so that, whatever time his boss arrived the next day, he would think he was in. This resulted in a game, in which Clive's manager did not gain anything.

If the boss had been more assertive he could have said something like, 'I would appreciate some more help. Would you please come in earlier?' This would have produced the outcome that the manager really wanted, and the overload of work would have been dealt with. However, Clive's manager was driven by 'Be strong' – he considered that it would be weak to ask for help. This syndrome affects a lot of people, particularly those in 'executive' positions.

Games

Blame is another element of manipulation. Some people will resort to games in order to get themselves off the hook or to put down another person. Some blame games are described very well in Eric Berne's book *The Games People Play* (See Further Reading, p. 149). One of these games is Blemish; another is Yes, But.

Blemish is simply about creating a bad atmosphere around a person, for example, 'What do you think about Jane?' said by someone screwing up their nose – to indicate that they themselves obviously don't think too highly of her. Or

'Have you seen Barbara's shoes!'

'Well, Maggie isn't exactly a size 12!'

All these statements are designed to 'blemish' the other person. They are often unjustified criticism and aimed at an area you can't do too much about, like your appearance.

The Yes, But game involves asking people for suggestions about how to handle a problem and then responding 'Yes but . . .' to each idea. Here the player is trying to tell the person in a roundabout way that the player is in control. This results in the helper feeling 'small', because he or she cannot find a solution to the problem. Anything you can think of to help has, of course, already been thought of by them!

Changing the way we speak to others

Psychologists Amy and Thomas Harris, authors of *I'm OK, You're OK,* and *Staying OK*, had some interesting observations on how we behave after studying the way people talk to each other. They divided the way we communicate with each other into three categories and called these Parent, Adult and Child. We all have the ability to speak and act as a parent, an adult or a child:

Here's an example of people making the same request in the three different styles. Write in the box provided the response you would give to the statement, and see if you can decide what the differences are.

Parent: It's about time you tidied up your socks.

```



```

Adult: Would you please pick up your socks.

```



```

Child: I'm just about sick of seeing your socks lying around.

```



```

What it is to feel like a child

However good a child may feel about themselves, they are small and totally dependent on their parents. All the situations that brought good feelings as a child could be ended by adults insisting on bedtime. So the child is reliant upon their parents for a 'happy childhood'. As children we all feel powerless, and these feelings can easily be reproduced when we feel submissive. The Harrises describe these feelings as 'I'm not OK, you're OK' feelings. However they do acknowledge that many children can be more confident and more assertive than others, but that this is due to them receiving unconditional love.

When we feel helpless or dependent on others, then we can recall the 'I'm not OK' feelings. Examples of this are when we are down on our luck, have no money, are sick, misunderstood, in a corner or just feeling old. These feelings of being out of control can lead to inappropriate behaviour – maybe submissive behaviour.

Acting the parent

The parent is the person whom we've copied, talking and listening to them all our lives. The influence of the 'parent' is very strong – parents tried to teach you the concepts of life. The parent in us judges people, particularly ourselves.

When you feel like 'beating yourself up', observe how you are acting at the time. It could be that you are playing the critical parent.

Parent-type behaviour is not always negative. We are also taught to be caring and nurturing parents. Likewise, childlike behaviour can also be free, fun-loving, intuitive and happy-go-lucky.

Being adult

The adult in us is the part that thinks things through rationally and considers the consequences of our actions. This part of us provides the means to work out how to do something. In fact, you were probably in your adult state when you bought this book to help you decide how to figure out the next stages of your life.

How you behave affects how others behave back

Often a 'Parent-type' statement will lead to a 'Child-like' response, e.g.
'Why don't you ever arrive on time?' (Parent)
'Because I've lost my watch.' (Child)
If you've understood a little about different types of behaviour, then you'll be able to answer the following questionnaire. Decide if the answer that the person gives is as a Parent, an Adult or a Child. Of course, a lot of the clues will not be available since you can't see the person's body language or hear their tone of voice:

Tick your response in the following situations:

1. A friend has just heard that they didn't get the job that they applied for.
    (a) 'Poor dear, you must feel terrible. I'll get you a cup of tea.'
    (b) 'That's nothing to worry about – you should have heard what happened at my first interview.'
    (c) 'I'm sorry to hear about your bad news. Let me know if I can do anything.'
2. One of your children loses a valuable watch.
    (a) 'You never look after things – go and look for it.'
    (b) 'Think about when you last had it and trace your steps back.'
    (c) 'I can't always be looking after all your property.'
3. The washing machine breaks down.
    (a) 'You kids have been touching my machine again, and now it's broken!'
    (b) 'I'd like to throw this machine out the window, it's always breaking down.'
    (c) 'I'll see if I can get the service engineer out this morning.'
4. Somebody brings you rumours about a friend's love affair.
    (a) 'Tell me more about that. I'd like to get something on her – she's always spreading rumours about other people.'
    (b) 'Let's not be too hasty and come to a conclusion before we've got all the facts.'
    (c) 'I think I should have a talk to Mary, she's got so many problems with her marriage.'

Now how did you do – look at the scoring key.

Scoring key

1. (a) P
    (b) C
    (c) A

2. (a) P
    (b) A
    (c) C

3. (a) P
    (b) C
    (c) A

4. (a) C
   (b) A
   (c) P

My Score

P = Parent
A = Adult
C = Child

The key to people's behaviour style is in the words they use, the sound of their voice and what you notice in their face and body language. The parent and the child both have a positive and negative side. We all know that parents can be authoritative or loving. The authoritative parent tells us that we should do things and judges us; the loving parent tells us not to worry and that they care. There is also a fun-loving child, as well as a defeated child, in us all. The fun-loving child is alive, hyperactive and assertively says, 'I want'; the defeated child complains, displays helplessness and says, 'I'll try' and 'Sorry'.

However, the adult in us all asks questions – generally open questions, like what, when, how, who and where. The adult asks for facts, thinks them through and makes decisions in a level-headed way.

We would be pretty uninteresting if we all behaved as adults all of the time, and it is our mix of behaviours as adult, child and parent that makes us interesting and unique. The key to success is to be able to recognize the different behaviours in yourself, to control them and to use this knowledge to develop your relationships.

What being assertive really means

This next section takes you through an exploration of what it's like to be assertive. It doesn't offer you a definition, but by the end of the chapter you should be able to give your own definition of what it would be like if you were more assertive.

The importance of self-esteem

To be assertive you need to have your self-esteem well anchored. This means you need to be able to say: 'I like myself.' However, if you've had years of not liking yourself for one reason or another, this can be very difficult.

Let's see how well you like yourself. Write down three things you like about yourself:

1.
2.
3.

Many women have a lot of trouble just writing one thing, and how many of you didn't write anything down at all? You just thought about it? Do you love and respect yourself enough to be able to read it in front of you on paper?

If you're stuck, here's some help. You can write:

- I am LOVING (we're all loving in our own special way).
- I am INTELLIGENT (everyone is intelligent). Yes, that does include you – it doesn't mean you have to have examinations to prove it.
- I have ENERGY (we all do so many things in a day).
- I am POWERFUL (we are all powerful people – we learn our power from when we are babies. We were helpless but spurred our mothers into action with our cries for milk or affection, and through our lives we learn how to get what we want from our parents, partners or children.)

These are qualities we all have. However we don't always acknowledge them in ourselves, perhaps because we have been hurt from a past experience. One way of breaking through the barriers you may have put up to appreciating yourself fully is to play Boast. With a group of people you 'boast' about all the ways you like yourself. You can get more and more outrageous if you wish. Here's what some women in one group came up with.

I like myself because:

- I'm honest and trustworthy
- I have a lot of warmth
- I'm persevering
- I'm caring
- I'm reliable, patient and hard-working
- I have a sense of humour
- I'm fit and healthy

- I bounce back
- I care about other people
- I'm a great lover!

Now you just keep going with your positive ideas about yourself.

-
-
-
-
-

The importance of liking yourself is that you don't need the approval of other people – you don't need other people to tell you that you are a good person, a caring mum, an intelligent member of staff, a considerate daughter, etc. Being able to praise yourself will give you power and control over your own life.

Enjoying rewards

Following on from giving yourself praise is the idea of giving yourself credit and rewards. Rewards are often only valued if they come from other people, but in fact they can be much nicer and more appropriate if they come from you. One of my rewards is a long bath one evening a week. Whilst I am there I eat something really special! And sometimes I build in a Sunday walk, something I really enjoy, to reward myself for a 'hard' week!

A friend of mine is very adept at this. One reward she decided for herself was her hour of 'p and q' on a Sunday. This was her weekly reward for being a mum. The 'p and q' stands for 'peace and quiet', and it meant that she could be totally on her own. Her husband and children respected her privacy at this time and did not interrupt it with trivial enquiries like: 'Where's my shirt?' or 'What's for dinner?' She chose to read or follow a hobby or go for a walk or just relax in the bath. This, of course, was not her only reward in life, but she made her hour a ritual that everyone observed and she derived a lot of pleasure from it.

Life is tough at times, and it's when it's at its toughest that we probably need and deserve some rewards. However, it's at these times that we are most punishing to ourselves. If we are working hard, then we drive ourselves harder; if we are lonely because of the break-up of a relationship, we isolate ourselves. That kind of behaviour reinforces an unhappy pattern which is unhelpful to us. Creating happy patterns, like rewarding ourselves, begins to make our lives seem more positive and, hopefully, enjoyable!

To build your self-esteem set yourself targets, and if you achieve them you can reward yourself with a treat. Some targets and rewards set by one group of women included:

Target	Reward
Getting the kids to school on time	Coffee with my best friend
Losing 2lb in two weeks	A meal out (not too many calories)
Writing my CV for a job	A cream cake
Telephoning my mother (with whom I've argued)	An hour to myself without the children on Sunday

Now set yourself some targets. Remember they must be:

- Realistic – i.e. not 'spend all my holidays in Hawaii' when you're living on a low income.
- Measurable – i.e. not 'be nice to my mother', because what is 'nice'? Telephoning her is measurable, because you know if you have done it or not!
- Achievable – make sure they are possible, i.e. not 'lose 2 stone in two weeks'.

It's time for you to have a go:

Target	Reward
1.	
2.	
3.	
4.	
5.	

Now think about taking control of your life and giving yourself rewards. Write down what you would like as a reward for sending off applications for further training or a new job.

- Spend a day birdwatching
- Have a slap-up meal out with friends
- An evening out with the girls/boys!
- A day out shopping and treating myself to some new things
- Your own idea _____

A reward needs to be something that you are in control of and you have the power to give yourself, rather than something that someone else can give you. 'Getting a job' is a bad example of a reward, because you do not have total control over it – it is in the hands of the employer.

Self-respect

If you are assertive, it means that you respect yourself and others. Respecting yourself means looking after yourself. It means, for instance, respecting your body and not abusing it, taking exercise and looking hard at your diet. People who live on the streets lose self-esteem. They have a poor diet and look bad, and gradually care less and less about themselves and how others see them.

Respect the decisions you make in your life. Remember not to put yourself down, also not to put others down.

Liking your negative qualities

Learn to accept your positive and negative sides. Instead of 'beating yourself up' for your negative points, consider liking them! Let's face it, we live with our negative parts and generally we may beat ourselves in public. But in private we are comfortable living with ourselves – we just don't always admit it to ourselves. For example:

- I like myself because sometimes I'm forgetful
- I like myself because sometimes I'm late
- My messy house shows some character!
- When I've had a few drinks I get a little argumentative. I enjoy them – it's fun.

Other people may not like your negative qualities, but *you* can. If you didn't like them, you would have used your power to change them.

Make a decision on whether or not you like your negative qualities. If you don't, change them.

Some of my negative qualities that I like are:

-
-
-
-

Some that I don't like are:

-
-
-
-

Criticism

It will help if you accept that we are all imperfect and that we all make mistakes.

Giving and receiving criticism is also part of being assertive. It is important, however, to give people clear instructions on how you want to receive criticism – for example, say to a friend, 'You can criticize what I do, but not who I am.' That means that when I've made a spelling mistake you can say to me, 'You've spelt that wrong', but not, 'You're stupid, you can't spell.'

Instead of giving constructive criticism we often call people names – 'Stupid', 'Fruitcake', 'Misery guts' and much, much worse! This is incredibly damaging. Tell people what they do that you don't like – so they can change. Likewise, ask people to tell you what is wrong so you can change what you do. But remember, you cannot change who you are – only what you do.

When you accept criticism from someone you also build a relationship with that other person. After all, it may have taken them quite a lot of courage to criticize you in the first place. Getting some information on our actions and the effect we have on other people can also be very useful feedback. We are not always aware of how we affect others or how they experience our actions.

Taking responsibility for your feelings

This is an important part of being assertive. It means not blaming other people about your actions and your feelings, for example 'You've upset me.' (You've made me make a mistake.) Taking responsibility would mean you would say, 'I felt upset when you didn't speak to me this morning.' Thus it was your decision to feel upset, and not someone else's.

Appropriate strategies

Being in control of your life doesn't mean you have to tackle every problem assertively. I have found the following chart helpful when describing 'appropriate strategies'.

HIGH

Smoothing	Assertive
Avoidance	Forcing

Need to maintain the relationship

LOW

Need to get what you want

Avoidance

The avoidance strategy can be used when assertiveness is hard work. If you have a low need to get what you want and a low need to maintain a relationship with the person involved, you can legitimately use avoidance tactics.

For example, if you bought some apples from a market stall and they were mostly bad and you already had a few apples at home and if, say, your bus had arrived, it might be perfectly legitimate to do absolutely nothing about the situation and avoid any discussion about it. In fact you could put the apples in the bin and forget the whole matter.

An example of my avoiding well is:

[ ]

Smoothing

If you have a high need to maintain the relationship and a low need to get what you want, you may decide the most appropriate strategy is smoothing, i.e. you agree with what is being said so as not to cause trouble. Excellent examples of this have been related to me mainly about mothers-in-law and other relatives! Can you think of any of your own?

An example of my smoothing well is:

[ ]

Forcing

If you have a high need to get what you want and a low need to maintain a relationship you can legitimately use forcing tactics. Here you tell people exactly what you want and why. Forcing will often involve a threat too, e.g.:

- 'If you don't put that cigarette out I shall call the guard'
- 'If you don't give me your car insurance details, I shall call the police!'

An example of my forcing well is:

[ ]

Assertiveness

If you have a high need to get what you want and a high need to maintain a relationship, then assertiveness is your only avenue. It means deciding what you need and how you feel. Many women feel that they should not have any needs and spend all their time looking after others, juggling time and not fulfilling their own needs.

Try to recognize your needs, and try to spend time fulfilling them or asking for them.

Expressing positive feelings

Once you have achieved your aim of being assertive, and people have perhaps carried out tasks that you have assertively asked them to do, you can show your appreciation. This is one of the skills of being assertive. For example:

- I appreciate your friendship
- I appreciate your encouragement
- I appreciate your stimulating conversation
- I really enjoy your sense of humour
- I like and appreciate your honesty and sensitivity
- I like you for your courage and ability to speak out in public
- I feel happy we share things together
- I've noticed your courage lately in not having a drink

Being assertive also means accepting compliments. An assertive person would reply 'Thank you' on receiving a compliment, rather than 'Don't be silly'.

Showing your appreciation

Exercise: Choose someone whom you have taken for granted, decide to appreciate them this week, and tell them that you do. If you are not sure how to do this, start by completing the following sentence:

> I haven't always told you this but I really appreciate it when you _____

If you can, be in touch with your feelings. It is even more powerful if you can say

> I feel _____ when _____.
> Thank you, I really appreciate it.

Someone may even give you some appreciation back, and say, 'Thank you for your appreciation, Linda.'

Using someone's name when you give appreciation is often a nice touch. But however you decide to give appreciation, always adjust it to your own personal style. By doing so, you will feel comfortable with whatever you say.

Disapproval needs airing too

The formula for addressing this subject is: 'I feel . . . when you . . . For example:

- 'I feel irritated that whenever I make a suggestion you say "Yes but".'
- 'I feel very angry that you've come to a conclusion about me without discussing the matter with me.'

Now think of something that you would like to communicate along these lines, and write your own sentence of criticism.

'I feel _____
when you _____.'

Setting limits

We also need to let people around us know where our boundaries are concerning how they should behave towards us. This means being able to say 'No', counteracting criticisms and put-downs and telling people how to treat you. You may need to confront someone's behaviour towards you, to change it. For example:

- 'I feel very angry that you always see me in the same negative way. I am not the person you think I am.'

People will push you all the time to test your limits. Children do this frequently to see just how far they can go. But you have the right to set limits concerning what you will do, as well as when and how you will do it.

Saying 'No'

Submissive people often feel that they are not nice people if they say 'No'. But this is not true. If you don't say what you feel, it is very unlikely you will ever get anything you really want.

As an example, let's say a friend asks to see you in the morning before work because she wants to talk to you. You are afraid to ask what it's about because you feel she must have a legitimate reason to see you urgently, so you stay home and are late for work. When she arrives it was a trivial matter, your day has been disrupted and you feel angry with yourself for not enquiring about *why* she was coming.

Has anything like this happened to you because you weren't able to say 'No'? Think about someone you'd like to say 'No' to now.

> Someone I'd like to say 'No' to now or more often is _____
> _____

One fear about saying 'No' is that you might hurt the other person. However, you can say 'No' without destroying someone. You can say it diplomatically and with love by telling them the reasons. The formula to use is: say 'How I feel'/ 'What I want to happen'. For example:

- 'I understand you want to pop round and see me, but can you tell me what it's about as I have to be at work on time?'

One woman had a friend who constantly let her down for appointments, a lunch, an evening out, by either not turning up, being very late or changing dates at the last minute. This was irritating, and to prevent it upsetting the relationship she would need to set limits. She could say, 'I feel I need more notice if you can't make it. Please let me know at least two days in advance so that I can make other arrangements.'

Exercise: Think about someone with whom you would like to set some limits. Write a sentence setting limits, using the formula in the box provided:

> I feel _____
> I would like _____

Initiating things

Being in control and being assertive also means being able to start things off – for example, being able to start a conversation with a stranger and expressing your opinions. If you have an opinion you have a right to express it – if you want to.

Accepting criticism

Accepting valid criticism is also part of this group of assertive actions. For example:

- 'I feel cross because I waited for you this morning and you didn't turn up.'

If this is a valid criticism, rather than make an excuse accept it, apologise and offer a reason – a true reason if you can. Don't, for example, make up a story like

- 'The bus was delayed in a five-mile jam. It wasn't my fault.'

What you are doing here is trying to blame other circumstances for your own delay. A true account might be:

- 'I'm sorry I'm late. I'll get up earlier in future and be more prepared.'

On the whole people will appreciate the truth much more and be more forgiving.

It is important that we accept our errors. However, we don't have to beat ourselves up about it when we are criticized. If you get stuck in submissiveness you will often seek forgiveness and try endlessly to make up for what you have done! Aggressive people, on the other hand, may deny the error and argue or criticize back in order to take the attention away from themselves. In both cases you will not feel good about the conversation.

If you deny the criticism, a vindictive person then has even more things to use against you! If you keep asking forgiveness, you may spend the rest of your life feeling guilty.

We all make mistakes. Admitting them will enable you to examine your behaviour and decide whether you want to continue it.

Making firm requests

When you want something, be specific about what you actually want and precise in laying down the details. Try not to use blame in saying what you need. A common example of not doing this well would be:

- 'I never get any help around here.'

A better way of being assertive and getting what you want would be to say:

- 'I'd like everyone to get into the habit of rinsing their own coffee cup after use and putting it away in the top cupboard.'

Being specific means not assuming that people know what you want. It may seem obvious to you that coffee cups belong in the top cupboard, but if people get into the habit of leaving them in the sink and you allow them to do that (even when it irritates you) it will be difficult to get them to change.

Here are some statements. Try to make them more specific:

'No one around here cleans up' (kitchen sink full of plates). *Write below what would be more specific*

```

```

'I'm always stuck at home' (you want to socialize).

```

```

'You don't seem to care if I'm tired' (there's a pile of ironing to be done).

```

```

Repetition can work wonders

When you really want to get your way, repetition can be a useful tool. For example, you take some cheese back to a shop and say, 'I'm returning this cheese because it's mouldy and I'd like a refund.' The reply may be, 'We don't give refunds.' Repetition is the key to changing the situation. Keep repeating, 'I'm returning this cheese because it's mouldy and I'd like a refund.'

You may get fobbed off with excuses four or five times, but if you can continue with the repetition in a controlled way without losing your temper, coupled with reasoning, it is a very powerful way of getting what you want. However, you must realize that here you are getting into the area of 'forcing', and that your need to get what you want should be stronger than your need to maintain the relationship with the person.

Children are excellent at repetition to get what they want. I once counted how many times my daughter Emma said, 'Mummy, I want some orange juice'. She was prepared to repeat it *ad infinitum* until she got what she wanted.

Throwing back other people's excuses

Very often people will give you invalid excuses for not doing what you want, e.g. 'You can't bring this back today because the sell by date is Tuesday.' Acknowledge that today is Wednesday, but tell them that you bought it on Tuesday and it is bad and you want a replacement.

You effectively repeat what they have said, agreeing with them, and then tell them what you want and expect and why. This tells them you are not arguing – you are willing to compromise and come to an agreement. Effectively you 'field' their excuse, just like being on a cricket field and throwing back a ball that's been hit towards you.

The formula here is to say: 'I understand that you [state how you think they feel] but I would like you to . . .'

Now try your own:
You can't go out with friends because of a commitment to your family:

'I know that you may feel _____
but I will _____ ,'

Acknowledging the feelings of others

If you want to maintain your relationships with people, you need to be aware of their feelings. For example:

I know you're going to be upset when I tell you this
BUT [tell them what you need] _____

or

- 'I understand that you might be disappointed that we're not coming over at Christmas, but I really would like to take a holiday away.'

If you can put yourself in the other person's shoes and think about how they might feel, it will certainly help if you let them know that. Expressing your own feelings will help too. For example:

- 'I will be sad that we won't all be together at Christmas, but I know that a holiday away is really what I need.'

Managing guilt

As part of the submissive, unassertive attitude which for centuries women have been programmed to adopt towards their families, it is very common for women to feel slightly guilty about their children, their partner or their parents. You name it and there's a woman feeling guilty about it! It's easy to *think* you are Superwoman and try to give everyone 100 per cent of your attention. In reality it's impossible.

What will you be feeling guilty about today? Here's a list of the some of the things women feel guilty about. Tick the ones you'd worry about.

	I'd worry about this!
1. The house is a mess. You invite a friend around. She arrives ten minutes after you get home.	
2. There is dust on a table and you see your friend looking at it.	
3. If you decided to employ a cleaner, you'd probably clean up first before they arrived.	
4. If your child is slow at school, you suspect it's because you are not with them enough or because you should have read with them more.	
5. You never get a moment for yourself because you never take a break from the children.	
6. You feel bad about having to take time off from work because of the children, e.g. sickness or a school function.	
7. Your aging mother complains she's lonely – you feel it's your fault.	
8. If you work you feel you are not a good wife because you're tired in the evenings.	
9. When household chores get left, you feel guilty you haven't done them because you consider it's your job.	

Well, how did you get on?

0–2 ticks	You are naturally a bit anxious about life – look again at the particular areas you ticked. Was it

- the home?
- the children?
- parents?
- work?

2–4 ticks   You are the average guilty woman! You are only guilty because you decide to be. Why not decide not to be?

4 ticks and over   You have pronounced yourself guilty. Probably everyone knows it and takes advantage of you in the areas where they know you are vulnerable. ('Would you look after my children while I go out and enjoy myself?' 'Would you take on extra work because I am tired?')

Well you can either keep putting up with it or tell others that they have to look elsewhere for help with their work or children – it's really up to you. Why not decide *not* to feel guilty, and have a little of what you want! For example:

I know I haven't given myself enough attention lately so I'm going to _____

_____

Body language

Body language – the way you sit and stand, your gestures and facial expressions – tells people what you really mean. Whatever you say to people needs to be reflected in your body as well as your tone of voice.

If your body language does not agree with what you are saying, you are giving a double message. For example, if you say, 'I feel really angry that you didn't turn up yesterday' with a smile and in a faint voice, it is unlikely the person will believe you. What's probably happening is that you are trying to tell them you are annoyed but also saying you still want them to like you at the same time. Many people feel afraid to say that they are angry and show it, and end up apologising for what they are going to say, for example, 'I hope you don't mind me saying this but . . .' rather than 'I feel disappointed/angry/taken for granted/cross.'

How assertive are you?

How do you feel about these situations/circumstances. Please tick.

		OK	Not OK
1.	Thanking someone for a compliment		
2.	Accepting a criticism from somebody		
3.	Confiding in a friend		
4.	Observing how other people react to you talking		
5.	Speaking up at a meeting		
6.	Saying 'No' to a favour		
7.	Laughing about your mistakes		
8.	Telling someone to stop doing something that is annoying you		
9.	Telling a loved one how you feel		
10.	Accepting someone saying 'No' to you		
11.	Complaining about the service in a restaurant		
12.	Walking into a room full of people		

Being assertive is possible, but it takes practice. Be prepared to 'fall off your bike' a few times whilst you are learning. Decide to be a winner and learn from your mistakes. There's no need to beat yourself up if you go wrong. Rather, sit down with a friend, and talk through what happened, and try to see how your behaviour may have contributed to their behaviour.

Here's a last exercise. Be brave and try and complete all the sections.

Areas where I would like to be more assertive are:

1.
2.
3.

Three things about myself that might get in the way of me being assertive are:

1.
2.
3.

Three things about myself that will help me reach my goals are:

1.
2.
3.

Notes on Chapter 5

6 Relationships

Making relationships work – both personal relationships and those in the workplace – is probably the most difficult area of personal success. This is because relationships rely very much upon the reactions and behaviour of the other person involved. The other person will often be very different from you and see things differently because of their experiences. We are all the sum of our experiences, and one person's interpretation of what you say will be very different from that of another.

In this chapter I have outlined some helpful techniques to help build relationships. Remember, though, that relationships need continual maintenance, like a car: they need to be worked upon or they go rusty or break down. It is very easy to take other people for granted and not to work on our relationships, but they do need continuous attention. They are often the most important feature of our lives, but very often the most neglected. Let's start by having a look at the skill of listening and how that can help in a relationship.

Listening alertly

Listening alertly is trying to *understand* what people are saying rather than just hearing the sounds that someone makes. It is a skill which can be developed – but it is not easy and requires a great deal of hard work.

What are the benefits of this hard work? Well, there are quite a few:

1. It leads to SOLVING PROBLEMS

If you listen long enough you will find things or ideas that you share. Building on the things you share will help you find a solution.

2. You get more INFORMATION and IDEAS
Listening shows respect, and when people are feeling good about themselves they contribute more ideas. When you are listening well there is less likelihood you will forget their ideas or opinions.

3. It cuts down on people TAKING OVER
Taking turns, with equal time spent on listening and talking, helps stop one person dominating the conversation.

4. It stops INTERRUPTIONS
If you take turns in listening to each other you will wait for the other person to finish before you come in. You know it will be your turn to talk in a few minutes, so you can put all your energy into listening rather than trying to spot a chance to throw in your contribution.

People sometimes fear that taking turns to listen will lead to long conversations. This tends *not* to be so, since people don't feel the need to keep reintroducing the point that no one listened to the first time, or the next, or the next . . . .

Formula for listening alertly

Pay attention
Allow plenty of time to listen. Pay good attention and show that you are listening by nodding and looking into the other person's eyes, but not staring.

Hold back your own ideas
Let the other person finish what they are saying. They will often utter the crucial part of what they are saying as a 'throwaway' line at the end. Summarize what the other person has said, to check that you understand.

Interest
Express your interest and encourage the person to continue.

Making sense
Help the person to develop and structure their idea. Summarize and agree the main points of what they are saying.

Allow silence

Let the other person have time to think and work out what they are saying. If the silence lasts too long for you to feel comfortable, repeat the last thing the person just said or say, 'I'm not sure how to read your silence' or 'Looks like you're having some interesting thoughts — would you like to say anything about them?'

Listening to someone else's problem

Good-quality listening is one of the best ways of working towards a solution for a problem. But the listener needs to observe certain rules strictly.

- Don't judge — never show any signs of your own feelings towards the person's problem. Remember you can show signs of judgement in terms of your body language (see p. 109) as well as with what you say.
- Look at the person — maintain contact with the eyes for as long as is comfortable, look away to the mouth when it becomes uncomfortable, then return to the eyes. Show interest with your eyes.
- Encourage the person to speak — when they stop or get stuck, allow them time to think and repeat back to them the last thing they said to help them find their flow.
- Help them be powerful. Many people can talk about their life but experience a total block about how to change things they don't like. Some helpful responses from the person listening are:
  (a) Ask the person what their best friend would advise them to do about the situation.
  (b) Ask them what they would do if they *did* know the answers.
  (c) Ask them what they would do if they were Superman or Superwoman.
- Get them to be specific, e.g. when they say 'I'd sort it out', ask them what specific actions they would need to take. Try to help them be objective and set themselves realistic, measurable targets.

Talking about relationships

When developing good relationships, too, it is important not to judge the other person too soon. Give them time, and then feed back to them how you feel about the way they are behaving towards you day-to-day.

Talking about how you are getting along in a relationship is going to help it to flourish and grow. There is a formula that will help if followed; however, it is difficult to develop the sort of relationship that is open enough to be able to discuss how things are going. You need to find your own level with the person, and they certainly don't need your comment on every single thing that they do. For instance, it is easy to get talking about relationships to extremes, and to end up analyzing or discussing how you're passing the marmalade to each other at breakfast!

We are sometimes scared that, if we tell the other person what we think, we may hurt that person. However, by keeping our thoughts to ourselves we are often depriving that person of information which could be very helpful. If we don't express the things that worry us our body language will almost certainly give us away, and to the other person this could certainly look like standoffishness or coldness.

Giving people the good news about themselves is often very embarrassing. However, if you deprive other people of your feelings of warmth and appreciation you deny telling them what you enjoy about being with them. If they don't know what they do that you really like, you leave them guessing. Most people would not be afraid to say if they preferred tea or coffee, a vegetarian or a steak meal. But often we are unwilling to let the other person know what we prefer or appreciate in their attitude and behaviour. If you are unwilling to do this, you are unlikely to get more of it.

So let's have a look at the formula that might be able to help us. If you ask people to describe the times in their lives when they learned something about themselves it is often when someone else told them about the impact or bearing they observed they had in a situation. However, this information needs to be given very carefully so that it doesn't anger or hurt the person.

Formula for talking about relationships

Tell with love
Don't start telling someone about the effect they are having on you when you are angry or feeling over-emotional. Wait until you feel some love and care for them, and be prepared to show it.

Be prepared to give your undivided attention, and listen carefully as you talk to the other person.

Tell how you feel
If you pronounce judgement on the other person they will just 'switch off'. You can't be the jury, either, and decide a punishment for them.

Developing a relationship by talking is about creating an atmosphere where you both can gain something.

Avoid being vague or too general.

Tell exactly the facts and how *you* feel.

Get the timing right

You need to time it as soon after the incident as possible, so that it's fresh in the person's mind. Storing things up will only lead to a build-up of anger. Little things left to build up cause long-term resentment, and this is very difficult to disperse once it is established.

Tell them how you'd like it

Make it possible for the other person to change what they do. Don't demand, make a request.

You also need to be prepared to listen to the other person in return and allow them to tell you things.

Ask how they're getting along

If you want to know how you're doing with the other person, you need to ask. They may not be used to telling you so honestly about how you behave, so take it slowly to begin with.

Check it out

Don't just listen and then go away without first checking that your interpretation of what the person has said is accurate.

Checking out how you talk about relationships

Here's a chance for you to assess how well you talk in relationships. The following questionnaire is designed to help you think clearly about the way you behave.

	How I talk		How my partner talks	
	Good	Needs to improve	Good	Needs to improve
Tell with love				
Tell how you feel				
Don't be judge and jury				
Get the timing right				
Tell them how you'd like it				
Ask how we're getting along				
Check it out				
Overall:				

Comments I'd like to make about improving the way we talk together in our relationship:

Understanding your feelings

It is essential to understand about how you think and feel in any situation if you are to communicate your wants and needs to others. Being in touch with your feelings is not always easy. Many of us have been hurt in relationships, and a frequent form of defence is to bury your feelings. This is no defence at all. Blocking your feelings will only serve to restrict the way to talk with a partner or someone else important to you.

First let's look at the different types of feelings we could experience. There are hundreds and hundreds of words that we use in everyday language to describe them. For example:

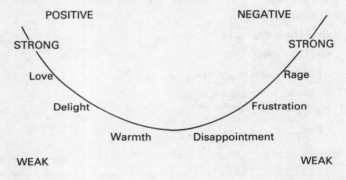

My feelings chart

Now spend some time, if possible with a dictionary or a thesaurus, making out a chart for yourself – exploring some of the feelings you experience.

POSITIVE   NEGATIVE

STRONG   STRONG

- - - - -   - - - -

- - - - -   - - - -

- - - -   - - - -

- - - -   - - - -

- - - - -   - - - -

WEAK   WEAK

Write words in the spaces that indicate your strongest positive feeling, then your strongest negative feeling. Once you've done that fill in your weakest positive feeling and your weakest negative feeling. Now fill in the gaps. When you've done that you should have some powerful words to use appropriately when talking about feelings in a relationship.

Good relationships at work

If we talk to people only enough to get the job done, we miss out on the added pleasure we can get from developing relationships at work.

We tend to make judgements about people at work from our first impressions. Early judgements are usually emotional and based around three areas:

- Do I like you?
- Do I rate you?
- Who's in charge?

Do I like you?
This feeling is based around many issues:

- Do I like the way you look?
- Do I like the way you speak?
- Do I like your mannerisms?
- Do you remind me of other people I like or dislike? (i.e. do you look like a schoolteacher I disliked?)

> **Write your own assessment here:**

There are more than a hundred variables that go to make up this initial decision. Most of them are usually based on inaccurate information that we have gathered about people. Some of the most common ones have sneaked into everyday language, e.g. 'Men don't make passes at girls who wear glasses', or 'Redheads are hotheads.'

Do I rate you?
This means, do I think you are competent and credible.

- Do you have a skill?
- Are you to be respected?
- What salary band are you on?

- To whom do you report?
- What sort of budget do you have?

```
Write your assessment here:



```

Who's in charge?

This third criterion is related to whether you feel this new person is friend or foe.

- Do they threaten you?
- How much power do they have?
- How will they use it?

```
Write your assessment here again:



```

In a study carried out of job interviews in America, it was discovered that most interviewers had made decisions about a candidate in the areas just mentioned within the first four minutes of the interview.

Actions can speak louder than words

How you act at work gives certain messages to all the people you work with. These messages are vital in influencing the reactions of others — the way you act will effect the way they act. For example:

- Nodding   gets you   more
- Disagreement   gets you   disagreements
- Judgement   gets you   resentment
- Smiling   gets you   smiles

Some actions improve relationships by creating a positive reaction from the other person. Other actions hinder a relationship by creating a poor reaction from the other person.

Decide your own actions

We all have a huge wardrobe of actions that we use in different situations. Just like throwing out old-fashioned clothes and hanging on to old favourites, we decide to stop using those actions that didn't get us what we wanted and to continue to use those that did.

As children we tend to work on this and practise asking for what we want at every available opportunity. However, when we become adults we tend to think we've learnt everything we need to know in this area and stop practising. Then when we have a difficult relationship at home or work it's easier to blame the other person than look at what *we* did. We have lots of off-the-cuff excuses for never changing the way we behave.

- 'You must take me as you find me' means 'I'm going to carry on and behave as I always do even if it doesn't suit you.'
- 'You can't teach an old dog new tricks' means 'I'm not going to change the way I do this.'
- 'I'll do it later' means 'Leave me alone, I can't be bothered.'
- 'I'm just like that' means 'I'm not even going to consider doing anything differently.'
- 'We'll see' means 'Probably not.'

What sort of actions do you think would help make a relationship work?

Make your list here:

1.

2.

3.

4.

5.

6.

7.

8.

9.

Here are some that are helpful:

- Smiling
- Looking at the person
- Nodding
- Leaning forward. But be careful here – different people have different 'social distances'. Middle Eastern people are comfortable talking to you as close as six inches away. Europeans are comfortable talking to you at anything from two to six feet
- Enquiring politely about their health, family, weekend
- Remembering things from previous conversations to show interest

Some of these things involve the way you behave and not just what you say. If your body does not mirror what you are saying, people will not believe what you are saying. To ensure that the body follows the words you must believe/feel what you are saying, in other words you must be genuine.

Learning to act effectively

Here's a formula to help you act effectively:

1. Write down the things you do that you think others may find unhelpful.

-
-
-
-
-
-
-
-

Give examples now of *bad* experiences:

Who was involved?
When?
The setting:

Unhelpful words you may have used:

Unhelpful body language:

2. Write down some things you do that may get in the way of a good relationship and that you could improve.

-
-
-
-
-
-
-
-
-

3. Why do these things occur?

-
-
-
-
-
-
-
-

4.   What do you gain from acting in this way? (Let's be honest, we don't do anything without some gain – so what do you gain from your negative behaviour?)

- •
- •
- •
- •
- •
- •
- •
- •
- •
- •
- •
- •
- •

How well do you get on with people?

Let's now look at how well you get along with other people Have a look at the list of everyday things in the questionnaire and decide which ones you need to do more of and which ones you need to do less of. Feel free to ignore those questions that don't apply to you.

Equally, there may well be things that concern *you* that have been left out, so use the blank spaces to write in your own ideas. When you have finished, go back over the whole list and circle those four or five things that you would like to work on for yourself over the next week or so.

For example, you may decide that you need to do more on listening. To help with this you could refer to the section on listening (p. 113) and look at some of the guidelines there.

My skills/abilities	OK	Need to improve

Talking and listening
Talking with more than one person
Sticking to the point
Making sure I am heard
Giving others a chance to speak
Listening well
Thinking before I speak
Keeping my contribution to the subject
  being discussed

Being alert
Recognizing stress in others
Observing which people speak the most
Knowing when someone loses interest in
  what I say and responding appropriately
Picking up the feelings of the other person
Noticing people's reactions to my words

Solving problems
Being able to state clearly what the problem
  is
Asking for ideas/opinions
Giving ideas
Weighing up ideas
Being able to summarize what's been said
Finding out more information

Keeping people interested at work
Showing interest in people
Bringing people who may be reserved into
  conversations
Helping people get on and share their
  differences amicably
Being able to use humour and fun
  appropriately
Sticking up for people
Saying thank you

My skills/abilities	OK	Need to improve

Knowing my own feelings
Telling others what I feel
Not becoming tearful or angry
Saying I don't agree
Saying how I feel when it's a good feeling
Thanking people
Not being sarcastic

Being in control
Calming anger
Accepting closeness and affection
Accepting silence
Accepting disappointment
Standing tense situations
Knowing what *I* want

Social relationships
Not putting others down
Not being too pushy
Trusting other people
Being helpful
Standing up for myself

Other
Understanding why I do what I do
Encouraging people to tell me what I do
    that affects them
Accepting help willingly
Making up my mind
Criticizing myself
Waiting patiently
Going off by myself to think

Notes on Chapter 6

7 Now You're Back at Work

So you've found yourself a job, and if all has gone well you're managing to balance the demands of the workplace with those of your family. You will probably have changed quite a lot, and you'll be pleased with those changes. But things don't stop there. You will need to ensure that you get job satisfaction, and problems can arise which will need to be faced. Several of the chapters in this book have had the aim of showing you how to deal with difficult situations and how to get what you want. This one contains some more useful advice at this particular stage.

The next section will also be very useful earlier, when you are merely thinking of returning to work. Before deciding which employers to apply to for jobs, think about the following questions. This will help you decide if you would really like to do what the employer has on offer. First gauge what you can from the way that the job is advertised. Next, when you apply for the job ask the employer to provide a job description that will answer most of the questions. Finally, at the interview check out your assumptions and fill in any gaps.

Defining your role

If you are working for someone, you will find life very frustrating if you do not have a very clear picture of your role, responsibilities and accountability. If the following questions have not been answered by the time you start your new job, make sure you have the answers as quickly as possible.

128

My job

Why am I employed? What is the main purpose of my job? Try to write a couple of paragraphs here about why the job exists.

What are the five main things that I should do (objectives)?

1.

2.

3.

4.

5.

What things should I do to be able to complete Objective 1?

1.

2.

3.

4.

5.

Continue to write these for each objective of your job.

Some jobs are pretty ill-defined. Complications arise when people don't understand what they should be doing at work. Often the boss will have a different expectation of the job from that of the person undertaking it.

The easiest way to resolve this is to write down what you think the job should be – as described above. Once you have completed this, you can discuss it with your boss and ensure you are both on the same wavelength. Don't get caught out!

Organizing your time at work

When you are working for other people it is really important to make sure that your time is managed well (see p. 14 for general assistance on time management). That way you can be seen to be doing a good job and will have more opportunity for improving your pay and possibly being promoted.

The next questionnaire is designed to help you look at your work and get clear in your head what you're meant to be doing and how. Try this exercise alone to begin with, then check it out with your boss so you can be sure that your assumptions are correct.

Many organizations have some form of appraisal system in which these areas will be covered. However, it is always good practice to think about these things first so that you are prepared.

Time-eaters

Lots of things take up your time at work. Which ones take up *your* time? Circle the ones that affect you.

What happens	Why
No one listens	Overloaded with work/information
Too much talking	Being bored. People not sure of what needs to happen
Hanging on to all the jobs	Fear of asking for help
Involving people who aren't 'involved'	Don't know where to look for help
Snap decisions	Not enough clear information or too much pressure
Jumping to conclusions	Misunderstanding vital information
Fear	Not enough clarity on what to do
Time estimates too short	Not negotiating properly
No planning	Unsure of your job
Not enough equipment	Lack of investment
Outdated procedures	Resistance to change
Can't say 'No'	Low self-esteem
Doing everything myself	Inability to delegate
Putting it off	Bored
Handling some paperwork over and over again	No set priorities
Others:	
●	
●	

So what's your contribution? Ask yourself:

- How am I involved?
- Am I the cause?
- Am I part of the problem?
- In what ways?
- When?
- Where?
- How?
- With whom?
- Why?
- How are other people involved?

- Are they the cause?
- Are they part of the problem?
- In what ways?
- When?
- Where?
- How?
- With whom?
- Why?

Is it caused by the way my job is structured?

- In what ways?
- When?
- Where?

- How?
- With whom?
- Why?

What part can I play in changing/improving this situation? Write your ideas here:

-
-
-
-
-
-
-
-
-
-
-
-
-

Being managed by a younger person

If you are returning to work in your thirties or later, it is very likely th
your boss could be younger than you. If you return to a 'youn
industry such as catering, retail or banking, he or she could be your
enough to be your own child!

People brought up and educated in different decades hold differe
social values and attitudes. Your opinions and ideas are likely to
different from those of a younger (or older) person.

Building a good relationship with your boss will be very importar
At best you could offer them your experience and maturity while th
offer their enthusiasm and energy. At worst they could be clumsy ar
inexperienced and you could be patronizing and condescending.

Stress and trauma

Stress and trauma are encountered both in domestic situations and
the workplace. If you're trying to combine both in your life the chanc
of your being hit by stress are probably higher – no matter ho
brilliantly you may have organized the family in your absence – and
is even more important to be able to deal with it.

Many women, through no fault of their own, appear to start off c
the wrong foot. Forty per cent of the women attending a Dow-Stok
Returners programme decide to come back to work because of
trauma. The most common of these is divorce. However, even a chi
leaving home or starting school can be a trauma for some women.

Getting help from the professionals

Most companies do not have the facility to counsel you at work. Mal
sure that you find out where you can get real help. Some useful peop
to call are:

- RELATE (formerly the Marriage Guidance Council; your loc
  number should be in the telephone directory)
- National Council for One Parent Families, 25 Kentish Town Roa
  London NW5 2LX
- The Working Mothers' Association, 77 Holloway Road, Londc
  N7 8JZ
- The Women Returners' Network, 100 Park Village East, Londc
  NW1

I went to talk to RELATE when I had problems with my own marriage. You can go on your own, and the woman I spoke to, who worked as a health visitor during the day, was very supportive.

The next step would have been to have got my husband to go along – but alas it was too late, which is why I had contact with the next organization, the National Council of One Parent Families. They publish very helpful literature about divorce and the various challenges you will face in being a one parent family. They are friendly and helpful and will talk to you sympathetically; although they don't offer the same sort of counselling service as RELATE, they offer more information.

The Women Returners' Network is a group of working mothers who got together to help women with the challenges of going back to work. They publish useful leaflets and information, and will be happy to talk to you about going back to work.

Once you are back to work or thinking seriously of returning, the Women Returners' Network puts you in touch with lots of other women in a similar position. They have regular regional meetings and publish a directory of members. The subscription is very reasonable, especially if you are not yet working.

What is stress?

Despite its bad name, we all need some degree of stress to function properly. When we talk of 'stress' what we usually mean is 'overstress'. It's this sort of stress that can cause heart disease. In the UK over 130,000 deaths per year are attributed to stress-related illness and over 40 million working days are lost because of it.

Your level of stress will depend on your level of physical and psychological activity – in other words how much your body and brain can take.

At low levels of stress you can become:

- Depressed
- Careless
- Accident-prone
- Fatigued
- Bored
- Frustrated

At high levels of stress you can become:

- Sick
- Irrational
- Panic-stricken
- Exhausted

At an evenly balanced level of stress your performance will be high and you will be:

- Creative
- Rational
- Problem-solving
- Making progress
- Satisfied

What causes it?

	Examples
• Achievement	Passing a driving test
• Threat/danger	Alone in a subway at night
• Boredom	No stimulation (ironing?)
• Frustration	Feeling you have no power/being unassertive/being ill in bed/dealing with bureaucracy
• Loss	A death/loss of something you treasured
• Physical problems	Unwell

These can all cause strain. The degree of strain will depend upon *you*:

- How you see things
- The number of stressful things happening at once
- How often it happens
- How long it happens for
- How hard it seems (jumping two feet or jumping ten feet)

Signs of stress

Physical

Dry mouth
Mouth ulcers
Stiff neck
Stomach-ache
Diarrhoea
Trembling

Headache
Migraine
Physical tiredness
Dyspepsia
Nausea
Skin disorders

Emotional

Temper
Not thinking straight
Tension
Tearful
Irritable
Taking tranquillizers or
   anti-depressants

Forgetfulness
Panic
Doing the unexpected
Quietness/feeling miserable
Nail-biting
Drinking

Relationships

Irritable
Impatient
Sharp and abrupt
Over-critical
Sulking
Strained – 'want to be alone'
Dependency

At work the signs of stress are:

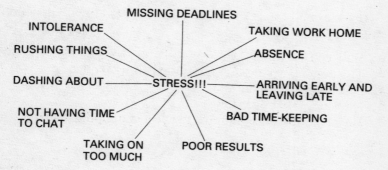

Keeping a look-out for stress

Watch for the early signs of stress in yourself and those around you. We often defend what we do in the most unusual ways – do you recognize any of these in you?

● Avoiding things	e.g. if you are drinking too much/avoiding sex
● Over-sharing	e.g. having exactly the same views as your partner or parents about things
● Going over the top	e.g. screaming at the kids over something minor
● Making excuses	e.g. excusing yourself for shouting at the babysitter – after all she *was* three minutes late
● Living in dreams	e.g. having to be fancied by every man around
● Child-like	e.g. not taking anything seriously (giggling a lot)
● Agreeing with everything	e.g. agreeing with everyone about everything
● Kicking the cat	e.g. blaming everyone else
● Being over-logical	e.g. it's only fair that you go on holiday without me, as you work and I don't
● Walking away	e.g. wiping your hands clean of an event

How stressed are you?

Put a tick in the column that applies to you.

	Yes	No
1. I have little patience with routine tasks such as washing up, filling in forms, etc.		
2. I hate queueing.		
3. I nearly always know what people are going to say and can finish their sentences.		
4. I'm always urging people to hurry up.		
5. I do everything quickly: walk, talk, eat.		
6. I'm impatient if things move slowly.		
7. I hate watching someone struggle with a job I can do more quickly.		
8. I often clench my jaw.		
9. I often rush through reading things and like to read just the summary – then can't remember what it said.		
10. I think about my work when I'm at home.		
11. I often turn a conversation around to my interests.		
12. I sometimes just pretend to listen.		
13. I feel guilty if I put my feet up and do nothing.		
14. I don't like slow drivers.		
15. Sometimes I grind my teeth.		
16. Often I just can't fit everything in.		

How to score
1 for each YES answer
0 for each NO answer

Results
How many ticks?

10–16   You are very stress-prone. You could be at risk of heart disease or other stress-related illness. You should think about counselling. Try to use some of the ways described to manage stress.

5–9   You are stress-prone. Again, you should look at some ways to manage stress.

0–4   You needn't worry at all about things being stress-prone – in fact you *don't* worry anyway!

Managing stress

You can do three main things:

- remove the stress: prevention
- Lessen the risk
- Plan to cope with everyday stress

Here are some ideas on how to counteract it:

Try some relaxation	See Chapter 2
Start a healthy diet	See your GP
Start a personal exercise programme	Try your local sports centre for advice on training and fitness
Make some time for yourself	See Chapter 3 (section on assertiveness, p. 96)
Show appreciation	Catch people doing things right
Set realistic goals	Make sure you can achieve what you set yourself in the time
Practise listening	See Chapter 4
Try counselling	Your local Citizens Advice Bureau will have a list of all your local counselling groups
Do some career/life planning	See Chapter 5
Take your mind off it	Take a walk or a break
Start a hobby	Contact your local adult education centre if you want to do it in a group
Let people know your needs	See Chapter 3 (section on assertiveness, p. 105)
Take up yoga	Try breathing exercises in a class; they are very calming and relaxing
Take a hot bath/shower	Or treat yourself to a sauna or even a session in a beauty salon!
Reward yourself	Love yourself, have a good time

Notes on Chapter 7

8 Learning and Growing – a Continuing Process

One of the activities that will help us to keep being successful is to keep on learning. For the successful person, a winning attitude means looking to learn something in all the everyday events that you encounter.

One of the most important areas to learn is about yourself. Someone once described this as sorting out the knots in the knitting and then taking pride in wearing the jumper. We have all got some 'knots in our knitting', and some of these knots create great holes in our jumpers which need attention.

In this learning process it's acceptable to remember that we are all imperfect. Trying our best is enough – we can't always expect to succeed fully every time. We can know that we have done our best and be willing to learn from our mistakes.

This chapter looks at some of the methods you can use to explore the kind of person you are. One of the most important factors in the way you deal with situations is your attitude towards yourself. The exercizes in the next few pages will help you to develop a more positive attitude towards yourself and your abilities, and thereby help you to achieve what you want.

How do you like to learn?

The way people prefer to learn varies. There are no right or wrong answers to these questions. The aim is to describe how you learn. Ring your personal response in each case.

A Think of some things that you have learnt in your life – for example, how to operate a new washing machine. If you were to have a new one delivered tomorrow, how would you like to learn how it works?

Would you:	Tick
1. Sit down and read the instructions fully.	
2. Ask the delivery man about how to operate it.	
3. Throw some washing in, press a few buttons and try it out.	

B If you were going somewhere new on holiday in the car, would you:

1. Just get in the car and go – if you got lost just stop and ask.
2. Get out all the relevant maps beforehand and plan out your route.
3. Telephone the AA and ask them to tell you the best route.

C If a new photocopier was introduced at work how would you like to learn to operate it?

1. Watch somebody before trying it out yourself?
2. Read the manual through first?
3. Try just to get on with it, and ask a question if you get stuck?

How did you score?

Doing	A3	B1	C3
Exploring/enquiring	A2	B3	C1
Remembering/thinking	A1	B2	C2

Doing

You are the kind of person who likes to get to the hands-on stage as soon as possible in the learning cycle. You are not content to sit there and listen and observe – you need to tell anyone teaching you something new that you learn best by getting involved.

Exploring/enquiring

You are the kind of person who likes to understand how things work and how they are put together. You need to ask questions as you go along.

Remembering/thinking

If you have picked all the answers in this section you are the sort of person who can watch somebody do it and then pick it up in a flash – or read the handbook and you're away. It takes a lot of skill to be able to learn in this way, although it is the way often taught at school – the old talk-and-chalk method of 'You listen while the teacher talks'.

Apparently inconsistent answers

If you've ticked a mixture of areas it could be that you just like to learn in lots of different ways. Just make sure that anyone who's training you doesn't restrict what you learn by not allowing you to practise, ask questions, observe and read alone for yourself.

Your attitude

What is an attitude? It can probably best be described as the way you are feeling and thinking when you meet any situation. Your attitude can be that of a winner or a loser. A winning attitude will be one that says, 'Today is going to be a good day and I'm going to achieve these things.' A losing attitude will be one that says, 'Today is going to be just as bad as yesterday – boring, hard work and uninteresting.'

The important thing to remember is that you control your attitude. So what's new about that? Nothing really – but it will have an effect on how successful you are. Your attitude is important because it shows other people how you feel. This physical and mental feeling affects:

- How you look
- What you do
- What you say

Finally, your attitude will affect how successful you are in achieving what you want and achieving the plans that you have already made whilst working through this book.

Do you take a winning attitude towards yourself?

	Yes	No

1. Humour
   Are you getting fun out of life and not taking yourself too seriously?
2. Learning
   Do you realize that to win you need to keep learning, especially from your mistakes?
3. Do you believe in yourself?
   Do you really believe in yourself as an intelligent, capable, loving, energetic person? Because you are – we all are.
4. Are you open to change?
   Do you try out new things, move on and try out something else if it is not successful, build on the things that go well?
5. Improvements
   Do you look at different ways of doing things and how you can make things easier and better?
6. Are you interested in other people?
   Do you listen?
7. Can you be a part of a team?
   Do you try to get to know and understand other people?

How can you develop a winning attitude?

Here are some ways:

1. Smile (even if you don't feel like it) – a smile gets a smile.
2. Be polite, but not submissive – remember to say, 'Do you mind if', 'Please may I' and, of course, 'Please' and 'Thank you'.
3. Develop patience – learn to accept that other people will never do things as well as you.
4. Share information – don't keep everything to yourself; there is no advantage to this.
5. Be on time and timely – it's good manners.

Being a winner at work

You can be a winner or a loser in all aspects of life, including work. A losing attitude says, 'What difference does it make if I don't do a job well?' A winning attitude says, 'I do my job as well as I can, so please respect me.'

When you return to work employers need your knowledge. What do you know about the job? Where did you learn it? How do you use it?

They look for people with lots of self-respect – people who will take pride in what they do.

They also want your reliability – they want to rely on you being there and to trust you to get the job done.

Next, they want your enthusiasm. If you are not enthusiastic about what you are doing, neither will the other people around you be.

If you have a positive attitude towards yourself and your work, it means that when problems come along they will be easier to handle, you won't give up too easily, and you won't feel sorry for yourself if things go wrong. Any mistakes you make will be less disastrous, and you'll be able to forgive yourself and accept that you are human after all.

If you have a losing attitude you'll be thinking things like:

- 'It doesn't happen anyway.'
- 'It won't happen to me.'
- 'If it happens it happens.'
- 'I'm going to keep to myself what I think and feel and let everybody guess.'

If you have a winning attitude it means that you will be able to think:

- 'I'll do my best.'
- 'I'd like to improve.'
- 'I'm willing to learn and listen to your ideas.'
- 'I'll be conscientious and careful.'

Influencing the quality of life

The quality of your own life will be influenced by your winning or losing attitude.

A losing attitude means that if you try something and find it doesn't work, you beat yourself up, give yourself a hard time and don't try again. As an example, take someone who tries to give up smoking and thinks that they have lost the fight completely when they want their first cigarette. Or the person who's trying not to drink so much and beats themself up when they slip back and get drunk!

A winning attitude would enable people in the same situation to think, 'Haven't I done well today? I've only had one cigarette. Tomorrow I'll try not to smoke any.' Or 'I had a binge last night and I've no excuse, except that I've got a terrible hangover this morning and I'll try again tomorrow.'

However, just having a winning attitude does not guarantee success all the time. Life is full of ups and downs, but you should enjoy it more if you are able to think about the good times and you'll feel better able to cope when the bad times are around.

Have I got a winning attitude?

	Yes	No
1. I am proud of how I look		
2. I am pleased with what I achieve each day		
3. I have a sense of humour		
4. I am always learning, especially from my mistakes		
5. I believe in myself		
6. I like to try new things		
7. I welcome positive changes		
8. If things go badly, I move on to the next thing and don't beat myself up		
9. I look for better ways of doing things		
10. I am always interested in others		
11. I like to listen to other people		
12. I can work as part of a team		
13. I can raise a smile – even on a difficult day		
14. I feel I am polite		
15. I don't keep everything just to myself		
16. I like to be on time		
17. I care about the quality of jobs I do		
18. I take pride in my work/leisure activities		
19. I am reliable		
20. I am enthusiastic		
21. I can forgive my mistakes		
22. I keep at it – whatever it is – and don't give up too easily		
23. When the going gets tough the tough get going, and that's me		

Well, how did you do?

20 or more Yes answers	You really have that winning attitude. You know you can do it . . . get out there and have it all!
10–20 Yes answers	You are well on the way to developing that winning attitude. Have a look at those areas where you said 'No'. Are there any circumstances when your answer would have been 'Yes'? If so, can you create more of those circumstances in your life?
0–10 Yes answers	So what's really wrong? You are obviously feeling down or doubting your abilities. Maybe you have had a real setback that's knocked your self-esteem. But the fact that you've had a go at the questionnaire means that you are at least beginning to think a little positively. Think about where and with whom you feel most positive and try to create more of that in your life.

Becoming a winner – what I need to do now

Write some action points for yourself. They need not be too elaborate.

1.

2.

3.

4.

5.

6.

7.

8.

9.

10.

Well, how did you get on?

We'd like to hear from you with the results of how you got on and how this book may have helped you decide what you want to do. Please let us know a little bit about you, your personal circumstances, how you scored and what course, job or career you are now following. Write to:

Linda Stoker
Dow-Stoker Ltd
The Mill
Stortford Road
Hatfield Heath
Bishops Stortford
Herts
CM22 7DL.

Further Reading

Directory of Further Education.
>From the Careers Research Advisory Council. A book well worth looking through at the library.

The Open Learning Directory.
>Catalogue of distance learning and independent study materials from basic courses to higher qualifications. It is a clear, concise directory covering an enormous range of subjects.

The Report by the Hansard Commission on Women at the Top.
>This report, published in January 1990, should be available from libraries. It makes interesting reading on the barriers to equality, and on where women are in the public realm and corporate management as well as in other key areas of influence. It then points out some strategies for change. Available from the Hansard Society for Parliamentary Government, 16 Gower Street, London WC1E 6DP.

Women Directors: a directory of the leading businesswomen in the UK.
>Some women directors will be well worth writing to for on-spec jobs. This directory says who they are, where they live and what they do. It should be available from reference libraries. Available from Eurofi (UK) Ltd., Guild Gate House, Pelican Lane, Newbury, Berks RJ13 1NX.

Women – the Way Ahead.
>Contains a workbook, consignment booklet, video and audio tape. Helps you look at extending your life beyond the home and contains some useful self-assessment exercises. Available from the Open College.

Bagnall, Nicholas, *Parent Power.*
>Concisely outlines the rights of parents and children within the education system.

Berne, Eric, *Games People Play.*
> Looks at the psychology of human relationships by analyzing the games that we play. He describes a number of life and marital games that we use from 'ain't it awful' to 'kick me – see what you made me do' and more interesting titles. As Berne is a psychiatrist, in some places the book is a little analytical and difficult to read, but worth persevering with.

Bolles, Richard Nelson, *What Colour is Your Parachute?*
> Take this one on holiday – it takes a while to read. Although it's an American book it makes fascinating reading for job hunters and career changers.

Chapman, Jane, *Women Working It Out.*
> Covers job search and the economic costs of returning to work and has a useful careers index.

Collins, Eliza G. C., *Dearest Amanda.*
> Letters from a businesswoman to her daughter give an insight into being back at work near the top, combined with some touching human insights.

Cooper, Carey L. and Marilyn Davison, *Women in Management.*
> Enumerates the difficulties that women are having in management, and shows how organizations can help develop their women to get the best from them.

Cooper, Henry, *Get Fit For Life.*
> This book has some useful tips like a traffic light guide to food; he talks about 'you are what you eat' and suggests simple exercises.

Dix, Carol, *Working Mother – You, Your Career, Your Child.*
> Carol Dix is an interesting and fluent writer who interviewed over 150 career mothers who are successfully developing their careers and at the same time fulfilling their roles as mothers. She tackles this difficult subject by writing up inspiring case studies on particular women. Well worth a read.

Dowding, Howard and Sheila Boyce, *Getting the Job You Want.*
> Useful advice for people looking for jobs in professions or growing careers.

Employment Department/*Woman's Hour*/Radio Four 1990, *Back To the Future.*
> Covers every aspect of returning to work – where are you now, marketing yourself, training and education, childcare, money, your rights and many other useful facts.

Freudenberger, Dr H. J., *Burnout.*
> If you are suffering from stress you could well be burning out. This

book is for the tired, disillusioned and frustrated, the listless, the bored and those constantly seeking excitement. Some useful insights from America on how to manage stress and not burn out.

GLC Women's Committee, *London Women's Handbook*.
Gives information about services and facilities in London which women might use, covering advice on employment, unemployment, further education, children, careers, black and ethnic minorities, health, housing, voluntary groups and a wealth of other useful sections.

Goffe, Robert and Richard Scase, *Women in Charge*.
A book for the woman entrepreneur, it describes the experiences of a number of women who have started their own businesses.

Goldburg, Herb, *The New Male-Female Relationship*.
I enjoyed reading this book about relationships – the fact that it is written by a man made it even more interesting to me. It takes us from looking at the myths around men and women towards a balanced tomorrow. Well worth a read. Available from Co-Venture, 23 Chesham Street, London SW1.

Jackins, Harvey, *The Human Side of Human Beings*.
This book gives us all hope that we are human, loving, intelligent and successful. It introduces an original and powerful (if a little evangelical) approach to understanding and approving human behaviour.

Jamieson, Alan, *Your Choice of Degree or Diploma*.
A useful directory to look at in your library if you are thinking of returning to study. Available from the Careers Research Advisory Centre.

Jenkins, Marie, *Women and Money: the Midland Bank Guide*.
A publication explaining how the Financial Services Act affects women; useful for women in employment, running a business or running a home. Covers budgeting and loans, divorce and bereavement, insurance, pensions, employment, self-employment, benefits and tax, laws relating to women's finance, banking, buying a home, setting up a business and making a will.

Lamplugh, Diana, *Beating Aggression*.
Diana Lamplugh's daughter Suzy disappeared from work without a trace in July 1986. The book looks at fundamental lessons women can learn to help themselves beat aggression at work.

Munroe, E. A., R. J. Manthei and J. J. Small, *Counselling – A Skills Approach*.
If you want to know more about helping people to help themselves, this is a good book, written in readable language. It gives explanations, examples and exercises.

Parsons, Edward J., *How to Win at the Job Game (A guide for executives)*.
> Advises you on how to analyze yourself and work out what you want to do in your future career. Looks at preparing CVs and works on your interview technique.

Pates, Andrew and Martin Good, *Second Chances: Adult Education and Training Opportunities*.
> A really good directory of education and training opportunities. It will help you if you have missed the chance of higher education and want it now, want an interesting spare-time activity, have been made redundant or want to change your job/career, have never learnt to read, write or spell well enough or want to develop new skills for your job.

Sharp, Sue, *Double Identity – the Lives of Working Mothers*.
> Sue Sharp interviewed a number of mothers living in Britain, working on all sorts of different jobs. The book is a series of case studies which look at the women's experiences and the difficulties of combining home and work.

Women Returner's Network, *Returning to Work*.
> Includes a county-by-county directory of courses and training as well as lots of other useful information for the woman returner.

Video:

Many Happy Returners – Encouraging Women to Return to Work.
> This video, put together in 1990, shows five case studies of women discussing how they coped with balancing the family and work, and covers confidence building, childcare, training and money. Available from Royal Society of Arts, 8 John Adam Street, London WC2N 6EZ.

NO LIMITS

I'm thirtyish and single again
I'm sitting here alone
At least I've got the kids in bed . . .
Can't think of anyone to phone.

Caught sight of myself in the mirror today
I didn't mean to look
There was a pale strange woman there
A character from a book.

I need to shake off these bad feelings
The ones I have about me
I must get out and meet new people
I'll make a cup of tea.

I'll start a leisure interest
But what do I like to do?
The last fifteen years have been devoted
To caring for the kids and you.

I guess I could just try different things
Experiment with my time
I feel unfit – I'll start with that
Have an interest that's all mine.

Thirtyish and starting again
I think I'll start my career
I'm doing some things for me now
I *am* important around here!

I've met a new person today
I was surprised that person was me
In control, calm, loving and bright
And with *no limits* of my own to restrict me.

Index